FreeSWITCH Cookbook

Over 40 recipes to help you get the most out of your
FreeSWITCH server

Anthony Minessale

Michael S Collins

Darren Schreiber

Raymond Chandler

[PACKT] open source
PUBLISHING   community experience distilled

BIRMINGHAM - MUMBAI

FreeSWITCH Cookbook

First published: February 2012

Production Reference: 1160212

Published by Packt Publishing Ltd.
Livery Place
35 Livery Street
Birmingham B3 2PB, UK.

ISBN 978-1-84951-540-5

www.packtpub.com

Cover Image by Asher Wishkerman (a.wishkerman@mpic.de)

Credits

Authors

Anthony Minessale

Michael S Collins

Darren Schreiber

Raymond Chandler

Reviewers

Jonathan Augenstine

Eric Z. Beard

Hugh Irvine

Acquisition Editor

Usha Iyer

Lead Technical Editor

Hithesh Uchil

Technical Editors

Vanjeet D'souza

Prasad Dalvi

Copy Editor

Leonard D'Silva

Project Coordinator

Joel Goveya

Proofreader

Matthew Humphries

Indexer

Monica Ajmera Mehta

Production Coordinator

Arvindkumar Gupta

Cover Work

Arvindkumar Gupta

About the Authors

Anthony Minessale has been working with computers for nearly 30 years. He is the primary author of FreeSWITCH and Director of Engineering at Barracuda Networks. Anthony created and continues to run the ClueCon Telephony Developers Conference held every August in Chicago.

Anthony has extensive experience in the Internet industry and VoIP. He has contributed heavily to the Asterisk open source project producing many features that are still in use today. At Barracuda Networks, Anthony oversees the production and development of the CudaTEL PBX appliance that uses FreeSWITCH as its core telephony engine. This is Anthony's second book; he has also co-authored the *FreeSWITCH 1.0.6* book published by Packt Publishing.

I would like to thank my awesome family: my wife Jill, son Eric, and daughter Abbi, for putting up with the long hours and supporting me on my cause to revolutionize the telephony industry. I would also like to thank the open source community at large especially those involved in the FreeSWITCH project and I hope to see you all every summer at ClueCon!

Michael S. Collins is a telephony and open source software enthusiast. He is a PBX veteran, having worked as a PBX technician for five years and as the head of IT for a call center for more than nine years. Michael is an active member of the FreeSWITCH community and has co-authored Packt Publishing's *FreeSWITCH 1.0.6*. He resides in Central California with his wife and two children and currently works for Barracuda Networks, Inc.

I would like to thank first and foremost my wife, Lisa, my daughter Katherine and my son, Sean, who keep me going each day. I would also like to thank the many FreeSWITCH experts around the world who are so willing to answer technical questions: Michael Jerris, Moises Silva, Raymond Chandler, Mathieu René, Ken Rice, and many more. I would especially like to thank Brian K. West for patiently educating me in the ways of VoIP.

Finally, I give my continued thanks to Anthony Minessale. In addition to authoring an amazing piece of software he has graciously let me work closely with the very talented core FreeSWITCH development team.

Darren Schreiber is the CEO and Co-Founder of 2600hz. He began working heavily in open source voice with the FreeSWITCH project, where he engaged with Brian, Mike, and Anthony. His projects have since evolved into two enterprise VoIP platforms that allow a multitude of development of voice, SMS, and video applications to be delivered to customers. Darren's 15 years of voice and IT experience include developing multiple enterprise SaaS infrastructures for hosting and remotely managing IT, voice, and e-commerce services. Darren is a guest lecturer at major universities on VoIP technology and leads paid international VoIP trainings. As a serious telephony enthusiast since a young age, he has worked extensively with VoIP technologies. Darren graduated from Rensselaer Polytechnic Institute with a degree in Computer Science and Business Management.

Darren is also a co-author on the original FreeSWITCH Telephony Book.

I'd like to thank, first and foremost, the FreeSWITCH team. Without them, I wouldn't have been challenged with some of the most intriguing technology and people I've ever worked with. It has been a gift working with them.

I'd also like to thank my family and friends who have put up with my crazy work schedule and constant tardiness, and have helped provide funds and morale support for our work. Specifically my parents who demand a check-in on how things are going at least once a week. Thanks for everything.

Finally, I'd like to thank the open source community. Their tireless patience and countless selfless contributions are a constant reminder that the world is not an evil place, and that people are generally out for the greater good of society.

Raymond Chandler (**@intralanman**) has been working with, and contributing to, open source projects for over a decade. Raymond's VoIP experience started with a small CLEC/ITSP using SER for call routing, and Asterisk for voicemail and advanced services. After encountering limits in Asterisk and looking for features not easily found in SER, he moved to using OpenSER and CallWeaver (then known as OpenPBX.org). While that combination was better, Raymond still had not found his perfect solution.

In 2006, Raymond was introduced to FreeSWITCH. Since then, he's been using FreeSWITCH and regularly contributing to the community. Raymond is the author of mod_lcr and several utility PHP/perl scripts. Raymond now works with Anthony Minessale as a CudaTel Software Engineer at Barracuda Networks (**@CudaTel** and **@BarracudaLabs**).

In the spring of 2011, Raymond was among the founding members of the Open Source Telephony Advancement Group (**@OSTAG**), whose mission is to advance open source telephony to new heights by funding open source projects through funds received by generous contributions and grants from those who share the OSTAG vision.

I'd like to thank my loving wife, Samantha, and our children for their support while they get less time with me than any of us would like.

I'd also like to thank the countless volunteers that step up to help out in the FreeSWITCH and other open source project communities. It would be impossible to keep any project running without them.

About the Reviewers

Jonathan Augenstine, Telephony Systems Development and Operations.

After graduating from college in 1982, Jonathan spent 12 years working in the analytical instrumentation field developing and deploying equipment into electronics and disk drive analysis applications. He worked in applications, engineering, and software development, and as product manager on the team that developed custom wafer monitoring equipment that was incorporated into wafer fabs for Intel, DEC, and IBM.

The next 18 years saw Jonathan take a new career path. After leaving the analytical equipment business, he moved into software development in the telecommunications market developing firmware for computer based telephony hardware at Dialogic, a telephony hardware manufacturer. He led the software development team tasked with migrating the system software and firmware from Unix on to the Windows NT platform.

Through various employment and consulting positions following his experience at Dialogic, including positions such as VP of Engineering and Network Operations, Jonathan has been instrumental in developing and managing operations of services that have integrated the POTS network with next generation Internet enabled applications. These projects included developing and deploying an international conferencing application with local access on four continents that integrated with radio stations streaming on the Internet. Participated in integrating SS7 capability with database locating services to enable E911 services on the mobile phone network. Other projects included development and operations of fax, conferencing, and IVR services that were deployed by companies such as WorldCom, Qwest, and J2 Global Communications in domestic and international markets that scaled into high volume usage.

The most recent project that Jonathan has pursued is the design and development of new technology that facilitates connecting directly to the voice-mail platform.

Eric Z. Beard is the Chief Technical Officer at AutoLoop, a company that provides communications and marketing software to the automotive industry. He has more than ten years experience as a software consultant and development team leader, working at companies such as Brainbench, British Telecom, AT&T, and America Online. He uses FreeSWITCH as a part of an outbound IVR system in combination with Microsoft Speech Server to make customer service calls for auto dealerships.

Hugh Irvine lives in Australia and is the founder and past President of the Internet Society of Australia as well as the founding Co-Director of APNIC in Australia.

He has over 30 years experience in computing and network engineering. His principle area of expertise is in Internet engineering and operation. He has worked for many companies throughout Canada, France, and Australia. He is currently an independent consultant.

www.PacktPub.com

Support files, eBooks, discount offers and more

You might want to visit www.PacktPub.com for support files and downloads related to your book.

Did you know that Packt offers eBook versions of every book published, with PDF and ePub files available? You can upgrade to the eBook version at www.PacktPub.com and as a print book customer, you are entitled to a discount on the eBook copy. Get in touch with us at service@packtpub.com for more details.

At www.PacktPub.com, you can also read a collection of free technical articles, sign up for a range of free newsletters, and receive exclusive discounts and offers on Packt books and eBooks.

http://PacktLib.PacktPub.com

Do you need instant solutions to your IT questions? PacktLib is Packt's online digital book library. Here, you can access, read and search across Packt's entire library of books.

Why Subscribe?

- ► Fully searchable across every book published by Packt
- ► Copy and paste, print and bookmark content
- ► On demand and accessible via web browser

Free Access for Packt account holders

If you have an account with Packt at www.PacktPub.com, you can use this to access PacktLib today and view nine entirely free books. Simply use your login credentials for immediate access.

Table of Contents

Preface

"Now what?"

That was the question that Anthony Minessale, Darren Schreiber, and Michael Collins asked themselves after the successful release of Packt Publishing's first FreeSWITCH book: *FreeSWITCH 1.0.6*. They were all tired from writing a book while still maintaining their day jobs and attempting to have a life outside of work. However, all felt a sense of pride and accomplishment at having released the first published book about FreeSWITCH. None wanted to lose the momentum.

It was decided that another book would be a good goal; but what kind of book? After kicking around a few ideas amongst themselves and members of the FreeSWITCH community, it was decided that a cookbook style publication would be a welcome addition. Packt Publishing agreed. Eventually it was decided that the most economical approach would be to focus on five basic subjects that are common to most FreeSWITCH installations.

What this book covers

Chapter 1, Routing Calls; getting calls from one endpoint to another is the primary function of FreeSWITCH. This chapter discusses techniques for efficiently routing calls between phones and service providers.

Chapter 2, Connecting Telephones and Service Providers; telephones and service providers have specific requirements for connecting to FreeSWITCH. This chapter will assist in quickly getting your FreeSWITCH server connected to other VoIP devices.

Chapter 3, Processing Call Detail Records; Call Detail Records, or CDRs, are very important for businesses. This chapter discusses a number of ways to extract CDR data from your FreeSWITCH server.

Chapter 4, External Control; FreeSWITCH can be controlled externally by the powerful and versatile event socket interface. This chapter presents a number of real-world examples of controlling FreeSWITCH from an external process.

Chapter 5, PBX Functionality; most telephone systems have common features like voicemail, conference calls, faxing, IVRs, and more. The final and largest chapter in the book, shows how to employ all of these features in a FreeSWITCH server.

Who this book is for

FreeSWITCH Cookbook is written for anyone who wants to learn more about using FreeSWITCH in production. By necessity some of the information contained herein overlaps with what is presented in *FreeSWITCH 1.0.6*. However, the information is presented in such a way that you can get up and running quickly. The cookbook approach eschews much of the foundational concepts and focuses instead on discrete examples that illustrate specific features. If you need to implement a particular feature as quickly as possible then this book is for you.

Conventions

In this book, you will find a number of styles of text that distinguish between different kinds of information. Here are some examples of these styles, and an explanation of their meaning.

Code words in text are shown as follows: "Many of the techniques employed in the `Local_Extension` are discussed in this chapter."

A block of code is set as follows:

```
<include>
  <extension name="public_did">
    <condition field="destination_number"
    expression="^(8005551212)$">
      <action application="set" data="domain_name=$${domain}"/>
      <action application="transfer" data="1000 XML default"/>
    </condition>
  </extension>
</include>
```

When we wish to draw your attention to a particular part of a code block, the relevant lines or items are set in bold:

```
<include>
  <extension name="public_did">
    <condition field="destination_number"
    expression="^(8005551212)$">
      <action application="set" data="domain_name=$${domain}"/>
      <action application="transfer" data="1000 XML default"/>
    </condition>
  </extension>
</include>
```

Any command-line input or output is written as follows:

```
perl -MCPAN -e 'install Regexp::Assemble'
```

New terms and **important words** are shown in bold. Words that you see on the screen, in menus or dialog boxes for example, appear in the text like this: "You should see an application named **directory** in the list."

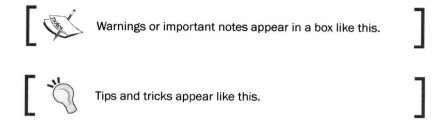

Warnings or important notes appear in a box like this.

Tips and tricks appear like this.

Reader feedback

Feedback from our readers is always welcome. Let us know what you think about this book—what you liked or may have disliked. Reader feedback is important for us to develop titles that you really get the most out of.

To send us general feedback, simply send an e-mail to feedback@packtpub.com, and mention the book title through the subject of your message.

If there is a topic that you have expertise in and you are interested in either writing or contributing to a book? See our author guide on www.packtpub.com/authors.

Customer support

Now that you are the proud owner of a Packt book, we have a number of things to help you to get the most from your purchase.

Downloading the example code

You can download the example code files for all Packt books you have purchased from your account at http://www.packtpub.com. If you purchased this book elsewhere, you can visit http://www.packtpub.com/support and register to have the files e-mailed directly to you.

Errata

Although we have taken every care to ensure the accuracy of our content, mistakes do happen. If you find a mistake in one of our books—maybe a mistake in the text or the code—we would be grateful if you would report this to us. By doing so, you can save other readers from frustration and help us improve subsequent versions of this book. If you find any errata, please report them by visiting http://www.packtpub.com/support, selecting your book, clicking on the **errata submission form** link, and entering the details of your errata. Once your errata are verified, your submission will be accepted and the errata will be uploaded to our website, or added to any list of existing errata, under the Errata section of that title.

Piracy

Piracy of copyright material on the Internet is an ongoing problem across all media. At Packt, we take the protection of our copyright and licenses very seriously. If you come across any illegal copies of our works, in any form, on the Internet, please provide us with the location address or website name immediately so that we can pursue a remedy.

Please contact us at copyright@packtpub.com with a link to the suspected pirated material.

We appreciate your help in protecting our authors, and our ability to bring you valuable content.

Questions

You can contact us at questions@packtpub.com if you are having a problem with any aspect of the book, and we will do our best to address it.

1
Routing Calls

In this chapter, we will discuss routing calls in various scenarios:

- ▸ Internal calls
- ▸ Incoming DID calls
- ▸ Outgoing calls
- ▸ Ringing multiple endpoints simultaneously
- ▸ Ringing multiple endpoints sequentially (simple failover)
- ▸ Advanced multiple endpoint calling with enterprise originate
- ▸ Time of day routing
- ▸ Manipulating To: headers on registered endpoints to reflect DID numbers

Introduction

Routing calls is at the core of any FreeSWITCH server. There are many techniques for accomplishing the surprisingly complex task of connecting one phone to another. However, it is important to make sure that you have the basic tools necessary to complete this task.

The most basic component of routing calls is the **dialplan**, which is essentially a list of actions to perform depending upon what digits were dialed (as we will see in some of the recipes in this book, there are other factors that can affect the routing of calls). The dialplan is broken up into one or more **contexts**. Each context is a group of one or more **extensions**. Finally, each extension contains specific **actions** that can be performed on the call. The dialplan processor uses **regular expressions**, which is a pattern-matching system, to determine which extensions and actions to execute.

To make the best use of the recipes in this chapter, it is especially important to understand how to use regular expressions and the three contexts in the default configuration.

Regular expressions

FreeSWITCH uses **Perl-compatible regular expressions** (**PCRE**) for pattern matching. Consider this dialplan excerpt:

```
<extension name="example">
  <condition field="destination_number" expression="^(10\d\d)$">
    <action application="log" data="INFO dialed number is [$1]"/>
```

This example demonstrates the most common uses of regular expressions in the dialplan: matching against the `destination_number` field (that is, the digits that the user dialed) and capturing the matched value in a special variable named $1. Let's say that a user dials 1025; our example extension would match 1025 against the pattern `^(10\d\d)$` and determine that this is indeed a match. All actions inside the `condition` tag would be executed. The `action` in our example would execute the `log` application. The `log` application will then print a message to the console, using the `INFO` log level, which, by default, will be in green text. The value in $1 is **expanded** (or **interpolated**) when printed out:

2011-01-09 13:38:31.864281 [INFO] mod_dptools.c:1152 dialed number is [1025]

Understanding these basic principles will enable you to create effective dialplan extensions. For more tips on using regular expressions, be sure to visit `http://wiki.freeswitch.org/wiki/Regex`.

Important dialplan contexts in the default configuration

As previously mentioned, contexts are logical groups of extensions. The default FreeSWITCH configuration contains three contexts:

▶ default

▶ public

▶ features

Each of these contexts serves a purpose, and knowing about them will help you leverage their value for your needs.

The default context

The most-used context in the default configuration is the `default` context. All users whose calls are authenticated by FreeSWITCH will have their calls pass through this context, unless there have been modifications. Some common modifications include using ACLs or disabling authentication altogether (see *The public context* section that follows). The `default` context can be thought of as "internal" in nature, that is, it services the users who are connected directly to the FreeSWITCH server, as opposed to outside callers. (again, see *The public context* section that follows).

Many of the PBX-related (Private Branch Exchange) features are defined in the `default` context, as are various utility extensions. It is good to open `conf/dialplan/default. xml` and study the extensions in there. Start with simple extensions like `show_info`, which performs a simple `info` dump to the console, and `vmain`, which allows a user to log into his/her voicemail box.

A particularly useful extension to review is the `Local_Extension`. This extension does many things:

- Routes calls between internal users
- Sends calls to the destination user's voicemail on a no answer condition
- Enables several in-call features with `bind_meta_app`
- Updates the local calls database to allow for a call return and call pickup

Many of the techniques employed in the `Local_Extension` are discussed in this chapter (see also *The features context* below for a discussion of the in-call features found in this extension).

The public context

The `public` context is used to route incoming calls that originate from outside the local network. Calls that initially come in to the `public` context and are treated as *untrusted*—if they are not specifically routed to an extension in the `default` context, then they are simply disconnected. As mentioned above, disabling authentication or using ACLs to let calls into the system will route them into the `public` context (this is a security precaution that can be overridden if absolutely required). We will use the public context in the recipe *Incoming DID calls*.

The features context

The `features` context is used to expose certain features for calls that are in progress. Consider this excerpt from the `Local_Extension` in `conf/dialplan/default.xml`:

```
<action application="bind_meta_app" data="1 b s
execute_extension::dx XML features"/>
```

This is just one of several features that are enabled for the recipient of the call. The `bind_meta_app` application listens on the audio stream for a touch-tone * followed by a single digit. The above example is a blind transfer. If the user dials *1*, then the command `execute_extension::dx XML features` is executed. In plain language, this command says, "Go to the `features` context of the XML dialplan and execute the extension whose destination number is dx". In `conf/dialplan/features.xml` is the following extension:

```
<extension name="dx">
  <condition field="destination_number" expression="^dx$">
  . . .
```

The dx extension accepts some digits from the user and then transfers the caller to the destination that the user keyed in.

This process demonstrates several key points:

- ▶ Calls can be transferred from one dialplan context to another
- ▶ The `features` context logically isolates several extensions that supply in-call features
- ▶ The `bind_meta_app` dialplan application is one of the means of allowing in-call features

Understanding that calls can flow from one context to another, even after they are in progress, is an important concept to grasp when addressing your call routing scenarios.

Internal calls

Calling local extensions is very simple once you know what needs to happen. In this case, we will review how to add a new user and make his or her phone available to be called.

Getting ready

If you are using the default configuration, then users 1000 through 1019 are pre-configured, both in the directory and the dialplan. To create a user outside this range, it is generally easiest to just run the `add_user` script, found in the FreeSWITCH source directory under `scripts/perl`. For example, to add the user 1020, launch this script from the FreeSWITCH source directory, specifying the user ID on the command line:

```
scripts/perl/add_user 1020
```

You can also specify a range of users:

```
scripts/perl/add_user --users=1020-1029
```

You will see a note about how many users were added. If you have the CPAN module `Regexp::Assembly` installed, then the script will also generate a 'sample regular expression pattern'. For our example, we will add a range of users 1020-1029.

How to do it...

Follow these steps:

1. Open the file `conf/dialplan/default.xml` in a text editor. Locate the `Local_Extension` entry:

   ```
   <extension name="Local_Extension">
     <condition field="destination_number
     "expression="^(10[01][09])$">

     . . .
   ```

2. Edit the expression in the `<condition>` tag to account for our new users. The expression pattern `^(10[012][0-9])$` will do what we need (look closely to see the difference). The new line will be as follows:

```
<condition field="destination_number" expression="^(10[012]
[09])$">
```

3. Save the file and then execute `reloadxml` from the `fs_cli`.

> **Downloading the example code**
>
> You can download the example code files for all Packt books you have purchased from your account at `http://www.packtpub.com`. If you purchased this book elsewhere, you can visit `http://www.packtpub.com/support` and register to have the files e-mailed directly to you.

How it works...

The `Local_Extension` is the default dialplan entry that allows directory users to be called. Remember, simply adding a user to the directory does not mean that the user can be dialed. (It does, though, usually mean that the user can make outbound calls.) So in order for your new user to be reachable, you need to add his or her user ID to the dialplan. By default, `Local_Extension` has a regular expression that will match 1000, 1001, ... 1019. When adding users outside that number range, it is necessary to modify the regular expression to account for those new numbers. In our example, we added user IDs 1020 through 1029, so we need to match those. We use this regular expression:

```
^(10[012][0-9])$
```

This matches 1000 through 1029. Let's say we added another block of user IDs with the range of 1030 through 1039. We could modify our regular expression to catch those as well:

```
^(10[0123][0-9])$
```

It is considered a best practice not to add a large range of dialable numbers in the `Local_Extension` without having the corresponding users in the directory. Doing so can make troubleshooting dialplan issues more difficult.

As a reminder, be sure to execute the `reloadxml` command each time you modify the regular expression (the changes you make to your XML configuration files will not take effect until they are loaded into memory, which is what `reloadxml` command does).

See also

▶ The *Creating Users* section in *Chapter 5, PBX Functionality*

Incoming DID calls

Phone calls coming in from the **Public Switched Telephone Network** (**PSTN**) are often called DID calls. DID stands for **Direct Inward Dialing.** DID numbers are delivered by your telephone service provider. They can be delivered over VoIP connections (such as a SIP trunk) or via traditional telephone circuits like PRI lines. These phone numbers are sometimes called "DID numbers" or "external phone numbers".

Getting ready

Routing a call requires two pieces of information—the phone number being routed and a destination for that phone number. In our example, we will use a DID number of 8005551212. Our destination will be user 1000. Replace these sample numbers with the appropriate values for your setup.

How to do it...

Follow these steps:

1. Create a new file in `conf/dialplan/public/` named `01_DID.xml`. Add this text:

    ```xml
    <include>
      <extension name="public_did">
        <condition field="destination_number"
        expression="^(8005551212)$">
          <action application="set" data="domain_name=$${domain}"/>
          <action application="transfer" data="1000 XML default"/>
        </condition>
      </extension>
    </include>
    ```

2. Save the file and then execute `reloadxml` from the `fs_cli`.

How it works...

All calls that come in to the FreeSWITCH server from outside (as well as internal calls that are not authenticated) are initially handled in the `public` dialplan context (dialplan contexts were discussed in more detail in this chapter's introduction). Once the call *hits* the `public` context, we try to match the `destination_number` field. The `destination_number` is generally the DID number (see the *There's more* section below for some caveats). Once we match the incoming number, we then set the `domain_name` channel variable to the default domain value and then transfer the call to user 1000 (FreeSWITCH is domain-based in a way similar to e-mail.

Most systems have only a single domain, although FreeSWITCH supports multiple domains. See the **FreeSWITCH** wiki for explicit information on multiple domain configuration). The actual transfer happens with this dialplan entry:

```
<action application="transfer" data="1000 XML default"/>
```

In plain language, this tells FreeSWITCH to transfer the call to extension 1000 in the XML dialplan and the default `context`. The `default` context contains the `Local_Extension`, which handles calls to users' telephones.

There's more...

Keep in mind the match in `destination_number` must match what the provider sends to FreeSWITCH, not necessarily what the calling party actually dialed. In North America, there are providers that send DID information in various formats such as:

- ▶ 8005551212
- ▶ 18005551212
- ▶ +18005551212

The expression must match what the provider sends. One way to accomplish this is to have a few optional characters in the pattern. This pattern matches all three formats listed above:

```
<condition field="destination_number"
expression="^\+?1?(8005551212)$">
```

The value `\+?` means optionally match a literal + character and the value `1?` means "optionally match a literal digit 1". Now our pattern will match all three formats that are commonly used in North America (technically, our pattern will also match +8005551212, but we are not concerned about that. However, the pedantic admin might be, so he or she can use the pattern `^(\+1)?1?(8005551212)$` instead).

See also

- ▶ The *Configuring a SIP gateway* section in *Chapter 2, Connecting Telephones and Service Providers*

Outgoing calls

In order to make your system useful, you need a way to dial out to the "real world". This section will cover dialing out to the PSTN and allow you to connect to land lines, cellular phones, and so on. In this recipe, we'll make an extension that will allow an outbound call to any valid US number. We'll attempt to complete the call using the gateway named `our_sip_provider`.

Getting ready

Making outbound calls requires you to know the numbering format that your provider requires. For example, do they require all 11 digits for US dialing? Or will they accept 10? In our example, we're going to assume that our provider will accept a 10-digit format for US dialing.

How to do it...

Routing outbound calls is simply a matter of creating a dialplan entry. Follow these steps:

1. Create a new file in `conf/dialplan/default/` named `outbound_calls.xml`. Add the following text:

```xml
<include>
  <extension name="outbound_calls">
    <condition field="destination_number"
    expression="^1?([2-9]\d{2}[2-9]\d{6})$">
      <action application="bridge "
      data="sofia/gateway/our_sip_provider/$1"/>
    </condition>
  </extension>
</include>
```

2. Save your XML file and press *F6* or issue the `reloadxml` command at the `fs_cli`.

How it works...

Assuming you have a phone set up on the `default` context, our regular expression will match any `destination_number` that follows the US dialing format (10 or 11 digits) and send the call to `our_sip_provider` in a 10-digit format.

There's more...

The regular expression matching in FreeSWITCH allows the possibility of having very powerful conditions. You can also match `caller_id_number` to route calls from a user at extension 1011 out to the second gateway called `our_sip_provider2` and everyone else at the `our_sip_provider`. Consider the following alternative `outbound_calls.xml` file:

```xml
<include>
  <extension name="outbound_calls_from_1011">
    <condition field="caller_id_number" expression="^1011$"/>
    <condition field="destination_number" expression="^1?([2-9]\d{2}[2-9]\d{6})$">
      <action application="bridge"
      data="sofia/gateway/our_sip_provider2/$1"/>
```

```
        </condition>
      </extension>
      <extension name="outbound_calls">
        <condition field="destination_number" expression="^1?([2-
        9]\d{2}[2-9]\d{6})$">
          <action application="bridge"
          data="sofia/gateway/our_sip_provider/$1"/>
        </condition>
      </extension>
    </include>
```

Note that we have two extensions. The first one tries to match the `caller_id_number` field to the value 1011. If it matches 1011, then the call gets sent out to the `our_sip_provider2` gateway, otherwise the second extension is matched and the call goes out to the `our_sip_provider` gateway. Note that we use $1 to capture the matching value in the conditions' expressions. In each case, we capture exactly 10 digits which correspond to the area code (three digits), exchange (three digits), and phone number (four digits). These are **North American Numbering Plan** (**NANPA**) numbers. The regular expression used to capture dialed digits will vary depending upon the country.

> Regular expressions can be a challenge. There are a number of examples with explanations on the FreeSWITCH wiki. See `http://wiki.freeswitch.org/wiki/Regular_Expression` for further details.

See also

▶ The *Configuring a SIP phone to register with FreeSWITCH* and *Configuring a SIP gateway* sections in *Chapter 2, Connecting Telephones and Service Providers*

Ringing multiple endpoints simultaneously

FreeSWITCH makes it easy to ring multiple endpoints simultaneously within a single command.

Getting ready

Open `conf/dialplan/default.xml` in a text editor or create or edit a new XML file in the `conf/dialplan/default/` subdirectory.

How to do it...

Add a comma-separated list of endpoints to your `bridge` (or `originate`) application. For example, to ring `userA@local.pbx.com` and `userB@local.pbx.com` simultaneously, use an extension like this:

```
<extension name="ring_simultaneously">
  <condition field="destination_number" expression="^(2000)$">
    <action application="bridge"
    data="{ignore_early_media=true}sofia/internal/
    userA@local.pbx.com,sofia/sip/userB@local.pbx.com"/>
  </condition>
</extension>
```

How it works...

Putting comma-separated endpoints in the argument to `bridge` causes all of the endpoints in that list to be dialed simultaneously. It sounds simple, however, there are several factors to consider when ringing multiple devices simultaneously in a real environment. The `bridge` application will connect the call to whoever sends media first. This includes early media (ringing). To put this another way, if you bridge a call to two parties and one party starts sending a ringing signal back to you, that may be considered media and the call will be connected to that party only. Ringing of the other phones will cease.

If you find that calls always go to a specific number on your list of endpoints versus ringing all numbers, or that all phones ring for a moment before ringing only a single number, your call may be getting bridged prematurely because of early media. Notice that we added `ignore_early_media=true` at the beginning of the dial string. As its name implies, `ignore_early_media` tells the `bridge` application not to connect the calling party to the called party when receiving early media (such as a ringing or busy signal). Instead, `bridge` will only connect the calling party to the called party who actually answers the call. In most cases, it is useful to ignore early media when ringing multiple endpoints simultaneously.

There's more...

In some scenarios, you may also wish to ring specific devices for a limited amount of time. You can apply the `leg_timeout` parameter to each leg of the bridge to specify how long to ring each endpoint, like this:

```
<action application="bridge"
data="[leg_timeout=20]sofia/internal/userA@local.pbx.com,
[leg_timeout=30]sofia/sip/userB@local.pbx.com"/>
```

In this example, userA's phone would ring for a maximum of 20 seconds while userB's phone would ring for a maximum of 30 seconds.

Call legs and the leg_timeout variable

The leg_timeout variable is unique in that it implies the ignoring of early media. When using the leg_timeout variable on each call leg in a bridge attempt, there is no need to explicitly use {ignore_early_media=true} in the bridge argument. For a more complete discussion of using { and } (curly braces) versus [and] (square brackets), see http://wiki.freeswitch.org/wiki/Channel_Variables#Channel_Variables_in_Dial_strings.

This method of calling multiple parties works well for small numbers of endpoints. However, it does not scale to dozens or more users. Consider using a FIFO queue in such an environment (FreeSWITCH's mod_fifo is discussed at length online at http://wiki.freeswitch.org/wiki/Mod_fifo). See also *Ringing multiple endpoints sequentially (simple failover)* for an example of ringing a group of endpoints one at a time, which includes an expanded discussion of using call timeouts.

See also

▶ The *Ringing multiple endpoints sequentially (simple failover)* section that follows

Ringing multiple endpoints sequentially (simple failover)

Sometimes it is necessary to ring additional endpoints, but only if the first endpoint fails to connect. The FreeSWITCH XML dialplan makes this very simple.

Getting ready

Open conf/dialplan/default.xml in a text editor or create or edit a new XML file in the conf/dialplan/default/ subdirectory.

How to do it...

Add a pipe-separated list of endpoints to your bridge (or originate) application. For example, to ring userA@local.pbx.com and userB@local.pbx.com sequentially, use an extension like this:

```
<extension name="ring_sequentially">
  <condition field="destination_number" expression="^(2001)$">
    <action application="bridge"
    data="{ignore_early_media=true}sofia/internal/
    userA@local.pbx.com|sofia/sip/userB@local.pbx.com"/>
  </condition>
</extension>
```

How it works...

Putting pipe-separated endpoints in the argument to bridge causes all of the endpoints in that list to be dialed sequentially. The first endpoint on the list that is successfully connected will be bridged and the other endpoints will not be dialed. There are several factors to consider when ringing multiple devices sequentially.

Notice that we added ignore_early_media=true at the beginning of the dial string. As its name implies, ignore_early_media tells the bridge application not to connect the calling party to the called party when receiving early media (such as a ringing or busy signal). Instead, bridge will only connect the calling party if the called party actually answers the call. In most cases you will need to ignore early media when dialing multiple endpoints sequentially.

There's more...

Handling various failure conditions can be a challenge. FreeSWITCH has a number of options that lets you tailor bridge and originate to your specific requirements.

Handling busy and other failure conditions

For example, when calling a user who is on the phone, one service provider might return SIP message 486 (USER_BUSY) whereas many providers will simply send a SIP 183 with SDP, and a media stream with a busy signal. In the latter case, how will the bridge application know that there is a failure if it is ignoring the early media that contains the busy signal? FreeSWITCH gives us a tool that allows us to *monitor* early media even while "ignoring" it.

Consider two very common examples of *failed* calls where the failure condition is signaled in-band:

- Calling a line that is in use
- Calling a disconnected phone number

These conditions are commonly communicated to the caller via specific sounds: busy signals and special information tones, or **SIT** tones. In order for the early media to be meaningful, we need to be able to *listen* for specific tones or frequencies. Additionally, we need to be able to specify that certain frequencies mean different kinds of failure conditions (this becomes important for reporting, as in call detail records or CDRs). The tool that FreeSWITCH provides us is a special channel variable called `monitor_early_media_fail`. Its use is best illustrated with an example:

```
<action application="bridge" data="{ignore_early_media=true,
monitor_early_media_fail=user_busy:2:480+620!
destination_out_of_order:2:1776.7}sofia/internal/
userA@local.pbx.com|sofia/sip/userB@local.pbx.com"/>
```

Here we have a `bridge` application that ignores early media and that sets two failure conditions, one for *busy* and one for *destination out of order*. We specify the name of the condition we are checking, the number of *hits,* and the frequencies to detect. The format for `monitor_early_media_fail` is:

```
condition_name:number_of_hits:tone_detect_frequencies
```

The `user_busy` condition is defined as `user_busy:2:480+620`. This condition looks for both 480 Hz and 620 Hz frequencies (which is the U.S. busy signal) and if they are detected twice, then the call will *fail*. The exclamation point (!) is the delimiter between conditions. The `destination_out_of_order` condition is defined as:

```
destination_out_of_order:2:1776.7.
```

This looks for two occurrences of 1776.7 Hz, which is a common SIT tone frequency in the U.S (there is a nice introductory article on SIT tones at `http://en.wikipedia.org/wiki/Special_information_tones`). If 1776.7 Hz is heard twice, then the call will fail as **destination out of order**.

When using `monitor_early_media_fail`, only the designated frequencies are detected. All other tones and frequencies are ignored.

Handling no answer conditions

Handling a no answer condition is different from busy and other in-band errors. In some cases, the service provider will send back a SIP message 480 (NO_ANSWER) whereas others will send a ringing signal in the early media until the caller decides to hang up. The former scenario is handled automatically by the `bridge` application. The latter can be customized with the use of special timeout variables:

- `call_timeout`: Sets the call timeout for all legs when using `bridge`
- `originate_timeout`: Sets the call timeout for all legs when using `originate`

- ▶ `leg_timeout`: Sets a different timeout value for each leg
- ▶ `originate_continue_on_timeout`: Specifies whether or not the entire `bridge` or `originate` operation should fail if a single call leg times out

By default, each call leg has a timeout of 60 seconds and `bridge/originate` will stop after any leg times out. The three timeout variables allow you to customize the timeout settings for the various call legs. Use `call_timeout` when using the `bridge` application and use `originate_timeout` when using the `originate` API. Use `leg_timeout` if you wish to have a different timeout value for each dialstring. In that case, use the `[leg_timeout=###]` notation for each dialstring:

```
<action application="bridge" data="[leg_timeout=10]sofia/internal/
userA@host|[leg_timeout=15]sofia/internal/userB@host"/>
```

Use `originate_continue_on_timeout` to force `bridge` or `originate` to continue dialing even if one of the endpoints fails with a timeout:

```
<action application="bridge"
data="{originate_continue_on_timeout=true}[leg_timeout=10]
sofia/internal/userA@host|[leg_timeout=15]sofia/internal/
userB@host"/>
```

Keep in mind that, by default, a timeout (that is, a no answer) will end the entire bridge or originate if you do not set `originate_continue_on_timeout` to `true`.

One other thing to keep in mind is handling cases where you are calling a phone number that has voicemail. For example, if you are trying to implement a type of "find me, follow me" and one of the numbers being called is a mobile phone with voicemail, you need to decide if you want that phone's voicemail to answer your call. If it does answer, then the `bridge` will be completed. If you do not want to have the voicemail answer and end the `bridge` (so that your `bridge` will keep dialing the other endpoints), then be sure to set the `leg_timeout` to a relatively low value. If the voicemail picks up after 15 seconds, then you may wish to set `leg_timeout=12`. In most cases, you will need to make several test calls to find the best timeout values for your various endpoints.

Using individual bridge calls

In some cases, you may find that it is helpful to make a dial attempt to a single endpoint and then do some processing prior to dialing the next endpoint. In these cases, the pipe-separated list of endpoints will not suffice. However, the FreeSWITCH XML dialplan allows you to do this in another way. Consider this excerpt:

```
<extension name="ring_sequentially">
  <condition field="destination_number" expression="^(2001)$">
    <action application="set" data="continue_on_fail=true"/>
    <action application="set" data="hangup_after_bridge=true"/>
```

```
        <action application="bridge" data={ignore_early_media=true}
        sofia/internal/userA@local.pbx.com"/>
        <action application="log" data="INFO call to userA failed."/>
        <action application="bridge" data={ignore_early_media=true}
        sofia/internal/userB@local.pbx.com"/>
        <action application="log" data="INFO call to userB failed."/>
    </condition>
</extension>
```

The key to this operation is the highlighted lines. In the first one, we set `continue_on_fail` to `true`. This channel variable tells FreeSWITCH to keep processing the actions in the extension even if a `bridge` attempt fails. After each bridge attempt, you can then do some processing. Note, too, that we set `hangup_after_bridge` to `true`. This is done so that the dialplan does not keep processing after a successful `bridge` attempt. (For example, if the call to userA was successful, we would not want to call userB after userA hung up.) You may add as many additional `bridge` endpoints as needed.

See also

> ► The *Ringing multiple endpoints simultaneously* and *Advanced multiple endpoint calling with enterprise originate* sections in this chapter

Advanced multiple endpoint calling with enterprise originate

You've seen many ways to ring multiple destinations with many options, but in some cases this is still not good enough. Say you wanted to call two destinations at once but each of those two destinations was a separate set of simultaneous or sequential destinations.

For instance, you want to call Bill and Susan at the same time, but Bill prefers you to try his cell first, then try all of his landlines at the same time. Susan prefers you to call her desk first, then her cell, and then her home. This is a complicated problem and the solution to that problem is called **enterprise originate**. The term enterprise is used to indicate an increased level of indirection, dimension, or scale. Basically, you are doing everything the `originate` syntax has to offer, but you are doing entire originates in parallel in a sort-of `super originate`.

Getting ready

The first thing you need to do to take advantage of enterprise originate is to fully understand the regular originate. Originate is the term used to indicate making an outbound call. Although there is an `originate` command that can be used at the `fs_cli`, the method by which you mostly use the `originate` command is with the `bridge` dialplan application.

The bridge application versus the originate command

Why do we talk about a regular originate when discussing the bridge application? Are not the bridge application and the originate command completely different? No! This is a common misconception, and it is incorrect. The bridge application is used in the dialplan, but it does exactly the same thing that the originate command does – it creates a new call leg. In fact, bridge and originate use *exactly the same code* in the FreeSWITCH core. The only difference between the two is where they are used. The originate command is used at the fs_cli to create a new call leg. The bridge application is used in the dialplan to create a new call to which an existing call leg can be connected or bridged.

You will need to open conf/dialplan/default.xml in a text editor or create or edit a new XML file in the conf/dialplan/default/ subdirectory.

How to do it...

The usage of enterprise originate is similar to the **ring simultaneously** example, but an alternate delimiter (:_:) is used:

```
<extension name="enterprise_originate">
  <condition field="destination_number" expression="^(2000)$">
    <action application="bridge"
    data="{ignore_early_media=true}sofia/internal/
    userA@local.pbx.com:_:{myoption=true}sofia/sip/
    userB@local.pbx.com"/>
  </condition>
</extension>

<extension name="enterprise_originate2">
  <condition field="destination_number" expression="^(2001)$">
    <action application="bridge"
    data="{ignore_early_media=true}sofia/internal/
    userA@local.pbx.com,sofia/sip/
    userB@local.pbx.com:_:sofia/internal/
    userC@local.pbx.com,sofia/internal/userD@local.pbx.com"/>
  </condition>
</extension>
```

How it works...

The entire input string is broken up into smaller strings, based on the :_: symbol.

Each of those smaller strings is fed to the regular originate engine in parallel and the first channel to answer will be bridged to the caller. Once one endpoint answers, the rest of the calls in the enterprise will be canceled.

There's more...

Enterprise originate has a few special aspects to consider when using it to place calls.

Setting variables

As you know, you can use the {var=val} syntax to define special variables to be set on all channels produced by originate and [var=val] to define variables per leg in a call with many simultaneous targets. Enterprise originate uses these as well, but remember that each string separated by the :_: delimiter is its own self-contained instance of originate so {var=val} becomes local only to that single originate string. If you want to define variables to be set on every channel of every originate, you must define them at the very beginning of the string using the <var=val> notation. This indicates that you should pass these variables to every leg inside every originate. Consider the following enterprise originate:

```
<action application="bridge" data="<ignore_early_media=true>
{myvar=inner1}[who=userA]sofia/internal/userA@local.pbx.com,
[who=userB]sofia/sip/userB@local.pbx.com:_:{myvar=inner2}
[who=userC]sofia/internal/userC@local.pbx.com,
[who=userD]sofia/internal/userD@local.pbx.com"/>
```

At first glance, this may seem confusing, but when you break it down, you can see what the values of the variables are for each channel. This table shows the values:

Channel	${ignore_early_media}	${myvar}	${who}
userA@local.pbx.com	true	inner1	userA
userB@local.pbx.com	true	inner1	userB
userC@local.pbx.com	true	inner2	userC
userD@local.pbx.com	true	inner2	userD

Once you know which syntax to use, it becomes a simple matter to set channel variables for individual legs, inside originates, or the entire enterprise originate.

Ringback

Unlike the regular originate, signaling cannot be passed back from one of the inner originates because there are too many call paths open to properly handle it. Therefore, when using `bridge` with the enterprise originate, you must define the `ringback` variable if you want to send a ring tone back to the caller.

See also

To learn more about originate and enterprise originate, look at some of the other examples in this chapter and study the default dialplan distributed with FreeSWITCH. There are several examples of the many things you can do when placing outbound calls found in `conf/dialplan/default.xml`.

Time of day routing

It is common for routing of calls to be different, depending upon the time of day or day of the week. The FreeSWITCH XML dialplan has a number of parameters to allow this functionality.

Getting ready

Determine the parameters for your routing. In this example, we will define business hours as Monday through Friday, 8AM to 5PM. Additionally, we will add a `day_part` variable to reflect morning (midnight to noon), afternoon (noon to 5PM), or evening (6PM to midnight).

How to do it...

Create an extension at the beginning of your dialplan by following these steps:

1. Add this extension to the beginning of your dialplan context:

```
<extension name="Time of day, day of week setup" continue="true">
  <condition wday="2-6" hour="8-17" break="never">
    <action application="set" data="office_status=open"
    inline="true"/>
    <anti-action application="set"
    data="office_status=closed" inline="true"/>
  </condition>
  <condition hour="0-11" break="never">
    <action application="set" data="day_part=morning"
    inline="true"/>
  </condition>
  <condition hour="12-17" break="never">
    <action application="set" data="day_part=afternoon"
    inline="true"/>
```

```
    </condition>
    <condition hour="18-23" break="never">
      <action application="set" data="day_part=evening"
      inline="true"/>
    </condition>
  </extension>
```

2. Later in your dialplan, you can use the variables `office_status` and `day_part`. `office_status` will contain either "open" or "closed" and `day_part` will contain "morning", "afternoon", or "evening". A typical usage would be to play different greetings to the caller, depending upon whether or not the office is open. Add these dialplan extensions, which will accomplish the task:

```
<extension name="tod route, x5001">
  <condition field="destination_number" expression="^(5001)$">
    <action application="execute_extension"
    data="5001_${office_status}"/>
  </condition>
</extension>
<extension name="office is open">
  <condition field="destination_number"
    expression="^(5001_open)$">
    <action application="answer"/>
    <action application="sleep" data="1000"/>
    <action application="playback" data="ivr/ivr-
      good_${day_part}.wav"/>
    <action application="sleep" data="500"/>
    <!-- play IVR for office open -->
  </condition>
  </extension>
<extension name="office is closed">
    <condition field="destination_number"
    expression="^(5001_closed)$">
      <action application="answer"/>
      <action application="sleep" data="1000"/>
      <action application="playback" data="ivr/ivr-
      good_${day_part}.wav"/>
      <action application="sleep" data="500"/>
    <!-- play IVR for office closed -->
  </condition>
</extension>
```

3. Save your XML file and press *F6* or issue the `reloadxml` command at the `fs_cli`.

How it works...

The **Time of day, day of week setup** extension defines two channel variables, namely, `office_status` and `day_part`. Note the use of `inline="true"` in our `set` applications. These allow for immediate use of the channel variables in later dialplan condition statements. Every call that hits this dialplan context will now have these two channel variables set (they will also show up in CDR records if you need them). You may have also noticed `continue="true"` in the extension tag and `break="never"` in the condition tags. These tell the dialplan parser to keep looking for more matches when it would otherwise stop doing so. For example, without `continue="true"` set, when the dialplan matched one of the conditions in the **Time of day, day of week setup** extension, then it would stop looking at any more extensions in the dialplan. In a similar way, the `break="never"` attribute tells the parser to keep looking for more conditions to match within the current extension (by default, when the parser hits a failed condition, it stops processing any more conditions within the current extension).

 A detailed discussion of dialplan processing can be found in chapters 5 and 8 of Packt Publishing's *FreeSWITCH 1.0.6* book.

Our sample extension number is 5001. Note the action it takes:

```
<action application="execute_extension"
data="5001_${office_status}"/>
```

This sends the call back through the dialplan looking for a `destination_number` of `5001_open` or `5001_closed`. We have defined both of those destinations with the extensions "office is open" and "office is closed," respectively. Now we can play different greetings to the caller—one for when the office is open and a different one for when the office is closed. As a nice touch, for all calls, we play a sound file that says, "Good morning", "Good afternoon", or "Good evening", depending on what value is in the channel variable `day_part`.

The execute_extension and transfer dialplan applications

These two applications both tell FreeSWITCH to execute another part of the dialplan. The primary difference is that `execute_extension` will return after executing another portion of the dialplan, whereas a `transfer` sends control to the target extension. In programming parlance, `execute_extension` is like a `gosub` command and `transfer` is like a `goto` command. The former comes back but the latter does not.

There's more...

You may be wondering why we did not simply use a `condition` to test `office_status` for the value `open` and then use `action` tags for "office open" and `anti-action` tags for "office closed". There is nothing preventing us from doing this. However, what if you need to have an office status other than "open" or "closed"? For example, what if you have an office that needs to play a completely different greeting during lunch time? This is difficult to accomplish with only `anti-action` tags, but with our example, it is almost trivial. Let's make it a bit more challenging by adding a lunch period that runs from 11:30AM to 12:30PM. We cannot use `hour="11.5-12.5"`, however, we do have another value we can test—`time-of-day`. This parameter lets us define periods in the day at a granularity of minutes or even seconds. The value range is 00:00 through 23:59 or 00:00:00 through 23:59:59. Consider this new **Time of day, day of week setup** snippet:

```
<extension name="Time of day, day of week setup" continue="true">
  <condition wday="2-6" hour="8-17" break="never">
    <action application="set" data="office_status=open"
    inline="true"/>
    <anti-action application="set" data="office_status=closed"
    inline="true"/>
  </condition>
  <condition wday="2-6" time-of-day="11:30-12:30" break="never">
    <action application="set" data="office_status=lunch"
    inline="true"/>
  </condition>
```

Notice that we need to explicitly define the weekend, since we cannot rely on a simple boolean open or closed condition. However, we now have a new `office_status` of `lunch` available to us. We define an additional extension to handle this case:

```
<extension name="office is at lunch">
  <condition field="destination_number"
  expression="^(5001_lunch)$">
```

Add the specific dialplan actions for handling calls during the office's lunch hour and you are done. You can add as many new office statuses as you need.

See also

Refer to the XML dialplan wiki page (`http://wiki.freeswitch.org/wiki/Dialplan_XML`) for more information on the usage of `break`, `continue`, and `inline` attributes.

Manipulating To: headers on registered endpoints to reflect DID numbers

Sometimes, when routing calls to endpoints that are registered to your system, you want to utilize custom To: headers. For example, if you are routing DIDs to a PBX or switch, the device you are calling might expect the phone number you wish to reach in the To: header. However, the customer or PBX may only have a single registration to your service that represents multiple DIDs that need to be routed.

By default, no flags exist to change the To: header to match the DID when calling a registered endpoint. Since the registration to your server is typically done via a generic username that is not related to the DID, you must program your dialplan to retrieve a user's registration information and parse out the username portion of the To: header, replacing it with your own. Care must be taken to replace only the username portion and to keep the remaining parameters intact, especially if NAT traversal is expected to continue operating.

Getting ready

Be sure that you have your DIDs and users configured. In this example, we will use testuser as the username with a phone number of 4158867999 and our domain is my.phoneco.test.

How to do it...

Create a dialplan extension, specifically for handling calls to the DID number and use some regular expression syntax to parse out the information. Here is an example:

```
<extension name="call_4158867999">
  <condition field="destination_number"
  expression="^\+?1?4158867999$"/>
  <condition field="${sofia_contact(testuser@my.phoneco.test)}"
  expression="^[^\@]+(.*)">
    <action application="bridge"
    data="sofia/external/4158867999$1"/>
  </condition>
</extension>
```

How it works...

You would typically make bridge calls to `testuser` using the `bridge` command with an argument of `user/testuser`. In this scenario, however, you wish to call testuser's registered endpoint but replace `testuser` with a phone number – `4158867999`, in our example. To do this, you must retrieve testuser's current dialstring and remove the username, replacing it with the DID number.

In the example, we leverage the `sofia_contact` API and some regular expression magic. The first `condition` simply matches the user's DID phone number—we only want to act if the destination number is `4158867999`. The interesting stuff happens in the second `condition`. The field is `${sofia_contact(testuser@my.phoneco.test)}`. By wrapping an API call in `${}`, the dialplan literally executes the API and uses the result as the field value. If we go to `fs_cli` and type `sofia_contact testuser@my.phoneco.test`, we get the result, which is something like this:

    sofia/external/johndoe@12.34.56.7;fs_nat=yes

The regular expression pattern `^[^\@]+(.*)` is applied against this value. The result is that everything after the `@` is placed in the `$1` variable. In our example, `$1` contains `@12.13.56.7;fs_nat=yes`. Finally, we execute the `bridge` with the dialstring `sofia/external/4158867999$1`. With `$1` expanded out, our destination is as follows:

    sofia/external/4158867999@12.34.56.7;fs_nat=yes

We have successfully replaced `testuser` with `4158867999` while preserving the necessary IP address and parameters for contacting the server and sent the call to the proper destination.

2

Connecting Telephones and Service Providers

In this chapter, we will cover:

- ▶ Configuring a SIP phone to register with FreeSWITCH
- ▶ Connecting audio devices with PortAudio
- ▶ Using FreeSWITCH as a softphone
- ▶ Configuring a SIP gateway
- ▶ Configuring Google Voice
- ▶ Codec configuration

Introduction

As its name implies, FreeSWITCH will "switch" or "connect" various endpoints together. Part of that switching involves making semi-permanent connections to individual telephones or telephone service providers. Service providers are usually telephone companies (telcos) or ITSPs (Internet Telephony Service Providers). Read on to learn about the many ways that FreeSWITCH can connect your telephone to the world.

The recipes in this chapter will delve into the various ways to connect FreeSWITCH to telephones and service providers. FreeSWITCH can also utilize a locally installed sound card by means of the PortAudio library. The last recipe is for advanced users and discusses the subject of codec negotiation.

Configuring a SIP phone to register with FreeSWITCH

SIP phones or any SIP device with the ability to register, are essential in most FreeSWITCH installations for allowing users to communicate with each other. A registration is when a phone or other device informs FreeSWITCH that it is active and provides information (such as an IP address and port) on how to reach the phone across the network or Internet. FreeSWITCH stores this information for use later if someone wishes to contact the phone.

In this recipe, you will be registering a phone to FreeSWITCH. You will need to enter your credentials into your phone as well as into FreeSWITCH itself (both sides must match). We will cover only the FreeSWITCH server portion of registration in this book.

Getting ready

Ensure the `mod_sofia` module is already compiled and loaded (Sofia is the SIP stack). You may also want to ensure the IP address your registrations are being accepted on for a particular domain name.

Follow these steps:

1. Launch the FreeSWITCH command line interface.
2. To view the current ports and IPs you are listening on, type:

    `sofia status`

3. Review the output, specifically lines listed as `ALIASED`:

```
freeswitch@internal> sofia status
Name                Type     Data                             State
=============================================================================
external            profile  sip:mod_sofia@192.168.0.100:5080 RUNNING (0)
my.company.com      alias    internal                         ALIASED
internal            profile  sip:mod_sofia@127.0.0.1:5060     RUNNING (0)
=============================================================================
2 profiles 1 aliases
```

The lines marked as ALIASED are DNS names that are recognized within the system and are used for registrations. Aliased DNS names are associated with a specific port and IP address. In this example, my.company.com is associated with the interface profile named internal. That profile listens on IP 127.0.0.1, port 5060. In essence, this means registrations to and from FreeSWITCH for my.company.com should occur on IP 127.0.0.1, port 5060.

How to do it...

The following steps will show how to configure an SIP phone:

1. Decide on a new username and password you wish to register with.
2. Open directory/default/USERNAME.xml in the FreeSWITCH configuration directory. Replace USERNAME with a name or extension number (such as 2000).
3. Add the following content to the file and save it:

```
<include>
  <user id="USERNAME">
    <params>
      <param name="password" value="PASSWORD"/>
    </params>
  </user>
</include>
```

   Replace USERNAME and PASSWORD in the code with a username and password of your choosing.

4. Load the FreeSWITCH CLI using.
5. Reload the in-memory configuration in FreeSWITCH's CLI by typing:

   reloadxml

You should now be able to configure your softphone or device to register with FreeSWITCH. To do this, set your username as USERNAME like shown, and your password as the PASSWORD within your softphone or device. Set your server to register to the ALIAS you identified earlier.

For example, if you created a user `1029` and password `PASS`, you would enter the following into your softphone:

```
Username: 1029
Password: PASS
Server: my.company.com
```

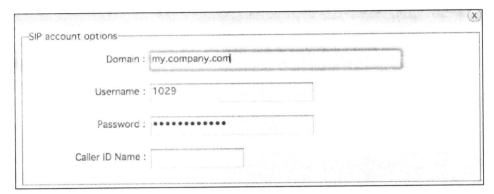

How it works...

Let's explain what you've done.

In the default directory, you've defined a SIP **Username** in the `<user id="">` field. This username is used for authentication of SIP packets.

You've added this option in a file within the `directory/default/` folder, which includes it as part of the default directory domain. That domain, by default, is your server's domain name (the `my.company.com` part—probably an IP address on your system).

There's more...

The SIP registration shown earlier was extremely basic. It doesn't set the Caller ID for the device/user, it doesn't specify a context for their calls to be placed in, and it doesn't add any extra variables to the account. Let's talk about these options as they are common additions to any registration and directory entry.

Caller ID

Using the previous example, suppose you want user `1029` to have a specific caller ID. You can make this happen by defining a variable within the directory section of a user's definition.

The example sets the **Caller ID Name** to "Mary Sue" and the **Caller ID Number** to "1029." Note that, if you choose to, you can override this setting within the dialplan—currently the directory entry variable is set when the call starts, but prior to the dialplan processing.

Customizing context

Calls received by FreeSWITCH will be directed to the context of the associated port and IP that a call comes in on, by default. For example, calls received on port 5060 that are authenticated are assumed to be from an "in-house phone" and get to use the `default` context. If, for some reason, you wish to override a particular device with a special context selection, you can do so by adding an additional variable:

```
<include>
  <user id="USERNAME">
    <params>
      <param name="password" value="PASSWORD"/>
    </params>
    <variables>
      <variable name="effective_caller_id_name" value="Mary Sue"/>
      <variable name="effective_caller_id_number" value="1029"/>
      <variable name="user_context" value="special"/>
    </variables>
  </user>
</include>
```

In the code, adding the variable `user_context` will route all calls from this device to the `special` context initially.

See also

Chapter 4, Getting familiar with the fs_cli interface

Connecting audio devices with PortAudio

Many of us have a USB headset or a sound card in our laptops or desktop computers. In most cases, FreeSWITCH can utilize these audio devices. Usually this is done for basic troubleshooting or to feed an external audio source into FreeSWITCH. It is also handy when you wish to use FreeSWITCH as a softphone, which is demonstrated later in this chapter.

Getting ready

The `mod_portaudio` module is already compiled for Windows users when using the Visual Studio 2008/2010 solution files with the FreeSWITCH source code. Linux and Mac OSX users will need to enable `mod_portaudio` in their FreeSWITCH installation. Follow these steps:

1. Open `modules.conf` in the FreeSWITCH source directory and remove the comment on the `#endpoints/portaudio` line. Save the file and exit.

2. Compile `mod_portaudio` using the following command:

    ```
    make mod_portaudio-install
    ```

3. If you want to have `mod_portaudio` load automatically each time you start FreeSWITCH then edit `conf/autoload_configs/modules.conf.xml` and uncomment the following line:

    ```
    <!-- <load module="mod_portaudio"/> -->
    ```

4. Save the file and exit.

5. If you do not load `mod_portaudio` automatically then simply load it using the following command from `fs_cli`:

    ```
    load mod_portaudio
    ```

Once `mod_portaudio` is loaded you are ready to start using the pa command.

How to do it...

The first thing to do is to become familiar with the pa command—pa being short for PortAudio.

1. At `fs_cli` type pa and press *Enter*. You will see that you have quite a few options.

2. To see a list of audio devices type pa `devlist` and press *Enter*. Here is the output for a Macbook Pro laptop with no external headset plugged in:

    ```
    freeswitch@internal> pa devlist
    0;Built-in Microphone(Core Audio);2;0;i
    1;Built-in Input(Core Audio);2;0;
    2;Built-in Output(Core Audio);0;2;r,o
    ```

    If you are using the standard speakerphone on the laptop then you are ready to make a call. If you have a USB headset, plug it into a USB port on your computer.

3. Type pa `devlist` again—note that the headset is not listed. Issue the command pa `rescan` and then pa `devlist`. Note that you now have a new device:

    ```
    3;Logitech USB Headset(Core Audio);1;2;
    ```

4. We need to tell PortAudio to use this headset as the input (i) device and the output (o) device. Optionally we can set it as the ring (r) device. The headset is device #3. Issue these commands to set it as the input, output, and ring device:

    ```
    pa indev #3
    pa outdev #3
    pa ringdev #3
    ```

5. Now you can make a call. Use the `pa call` command to send a call through the dialplan. Try calling 9196, the default echo test extension:

   ```
   pa call 9196
   ```

6. You should hear your voice echoed back to you. When you are done testing, hang up the call by issuing the `pa hangup` command.

How it works...

PortAudio allows FreeSWITCH to use local audio devices, such as sound cards and USB headsets, as endpoints. Some systems have more than one input or output device so it is necessary to specify which one to use by issuing the `pa indev`, `pa outdev`, and `pa ringdev` commands. Using `pa call` and `pa hangup` allows you to handle phone calls right at the FreeSWITCH command line.

There's more...

PortAudio can also receive calls on the `portaudio` channel. Try the following command from `fs_cli`:

```
originate loopback/9664 bridge:portaudio inline
```

The `portaudio` channel will "ring" and you can answer by issuing the `pa answer` command. You can eliminate the need to use `pa answer` by using the `auto_answer` option:

```
originate loopback/9664 bridge:portaudio/auto_answer inline
```

You can also use this technique to create a simple announcement system. You will need a second phone, preferably a SIP phone registered to FreeSWITCH. Connect a set of speakers to the appropriate output port on your sound card. If necessary, issue the `pa outdev` command to select the device to which your speakers are connected. Test the connection with the `originate` command. Assuming your SIP phone is registered as 1000, issue this command:

```
originate user/1000 bridge:portaudio/auto_answer inline
```

Your voice will now be heard over the speakers. You can also create a dialplan entry to accomplish this. Here's an example:

```
<extension name="portaudio test">
  <condition field="destination_number" expression="^(9908)$">
    <action application="answer"/>
    <action application="bridge" data="portaudio/auto_answer"/>
  </condition>
</extension>
```

This extension would allow you to dial 9908 and make an announcement over the speakers.

See also

▶ The *Using FreeSWITCH as a softphone* recipe that follows

Using FreeSWITCH as a softphone

The previous recipe described the process of setting up FreeSWITCH to use a local audio device such as a USB headset or a sound card. This recipe builds on the previous one by showing you how to use a custom FreeSWITCH configuration that is tailored specifically for use as a softphone (be sure to have PortAudio working before trying this recipe). Lastly, we will direct your attention to a few open source softphone projects that utilize FreeSWITCH as the VoIP engine.

Getting ready

This operation requires that we download a preconfigured FreeSWITCH configuration file. Follow these steps:

1. Stop FreeSWITCH with this command:

   ```
   freeswitch -stop
   ```

2. Back up your existing configuration (if desired). In a Linux/Unix environment a command like this would suffice:

   ```
   mv /usr/local/freeswitch/conf /usr/local/freeswith/conf.bak
   ```

   Windows users can use the **File Manager** to rename the `conf` folder.

3. You can retrieve the softphone configuration from the FreeSWITCH sample configs `git` repository with this command:

   ```
   git clone git://git.freeswitch.org/freeswitch-sample-configs.git
   ```

   This downloads all of the sample configurations, one of which is named "softphone". Copy the `softphone` subdirectory over to the installation directory (`/usr/local/freeswitch`) and name it `conf`.

4. The last step is to configure any gateways that you may have. These should be placed in `conf/accounts`. If you have already configured one or more gateways in your standard FreeSWITCH configuration you can simply copy those XML files into `conf/accounts` without making any other modifications.

5. Start FreeSWITCH in the foreground (do not use the -nc flag):

   ```
   /usr/local/freeswitch/bin/freeswitch
   ```

6. Use the `pa indev` and `pa outdev` commands to select your audio device.

You are now ready to try out the FreeSWITCH softphone configuration.

How to do it...

Simply make a call using the `pa call` command. The softphone configuration accepts a number of different dialstring formats. For simple testing use a simple SIP URI. Try calling the FreeSWITCH public conference server:

```
pa call sip:888@conference.freeswitch.org
```

Issue a `pa hangup` command to end the call.

How it works...

The softphone configuration is an example of a more streamlined FreeSWITCH configuration. It puts all configuration options into `freeswitch.xml` (except for your custom gateway files) and it loads only a specific set of modules. For example, it does not load `mod_event_socket`, which means you cannot use `fs_cli` (and thus why you must start FreeSWITCH without the `-nc` flag). Feel free to examine `freeswitch.xml`—it is less than 300 lines!

Here are a few more features to keep in mind:

- The softphone configuration accepts SIP URIs in the form of `sip:user@domain` or `sip:codec:user@domain`.

- The softphone configuration lets you call a phone number without specifying a domain name or gateway if you have configured a default gateway. For example: `pa call 18005551212`.

- If you have a single gateway and you would like it to be used for all outbound calls then modify the following line in `freeswitch.xml` to use the name of your gateway:

  ```
  <X-PRE-PROCESS cmd="set" data="default_gateway=default"/>
  ```

- You can customize your caller ID sending by modifying the following lines in `freeswitch.xml`:

  ```
  <X-PRE-PROCESS cmd="set" data="outbound_caller_name=FreeSWITCH"/>
  <X-PRE-PROCESS cmd="set" data="outbound_caller_id=0000000000"/>
  ```

There's more...

As of this writing, there are two projects in development that are softphones which utilize FreeSWITCH as the VoIP engine. The first one is called FreeSWITCH Communicator. It is found in the FreeSWITCH source tree in the `fscomm` directory. It is a cross-platform softphone based on Nokia's QT library. Visit `http://wiki.freeswitch.org/wiki/FSComm` to learn more.

The other softphone is Windows-only and is called FSClient. It can be found in the `freeswitch-contrib` git repository. Visit `http://wiki.freeswitch.org/wiki/FSClient` to learn more.

See also

▸ Refer to the *Connecting audio devices with PortAudio* recipe we saw earlier

Configuring a SIP gateway

Configuring a SIP gateway allows you to connect with outside carriers or other SIP machines. You can connect with other FreeSWITCH or Asterisk boxes, or to upstream carrier SIP trunks.

SIP gateways have many, many options—too many to list here, so we'll review just a few.

Getting ready

First you'll need to gather some information about the remote server to which you are connecting. The list generally includes:

▸ IP address or hostname of the server you are connecting to

▸ Username and password (if any)

▸ How the carrier/gateway expects Caller ID to be handled (which SIP header Caller ID should be placed in)

▸ Whether registration is required

You'll also need to know the phone number format your carrier expects when you send calls to them, and how they'll send calls to you.

Finally, you'll need to decide which of your existing SIP interfaces to tie this gateway to. All gateways must be associated with a SIP interface (port and IP address). Note that, in most cases, a gateway can be utilized on multiple SIP interfaces if desired.

Some carriers use SIP registrations to figure out how to send calls to you, while other carriers map IP and port addresses permanently to deliver calls to you. Some carriers also allow DNS based records to be used. You should find out what your provider utilizes, as you generally set these options within the provider's configuration interface and not FreeSWITCH.

How to do it...

Gateways are associated with SIP profiles because FreeSWITCH needs to know which IP and port to send traffic to and from in relation to the carrier.

First, you'll need to add a gateway to your SIP profile. Let's assume you're using the default FreeSWITCH configuration. In this case, we'll create a gateway that is attached to the default **external** profile.

1. Create a file in the `conf/sip_profiles/external/` directory named after your gateway (that is, `cheap_tel.xml`)

2. Add the following content (note that even if you are not registering, a username and password is required) but replace the highlighted items with your own provider:

```
<include>
  <gateway name="providerA">
    <param name="realm" value="sip.2600hz.com"/>
    <param name="username" value="darren"/>
    <param name="password" value="test"/>
    <param name="register" value="true"/>
  </gateway>
</include>
```

3. You will access the gateway by using the bridge application with `sofia/gateway/providerA/number`, such as `sofia/gateway/providerA/4158867999`. You can do this in any dialplan you are using. In this example, edit your dialplan (typically the default dialplan in `conf/dialplan/default.xml`) and add code to utilize the gateway:

```
<extension name="dial-10-digit-numbers">
  <condition field="destination_number"
            expression="^(\d{10})$">
    <action application="bridge"
           data="sofia/gateway/providerA/$1"/>
  </condition>
</extension>
```

4. Issue a `reloadxml` command in your FreeSWITCH CLI after making the mentioned changes.

5. Issue a `sofia profile external rescan` to instruct FreeSWITCH to find any new gateways or settings on the profile **external** and add them to the running stack.

Sofia profile rescan versus reload

When making changes to your SIP configuration files you will have to tell FreeSWITCH's SIP module ("sofia") that you want those changes to take effect. Simply reloading the XML configuration does not force `sofia` to apply the changes. Instead, you will need to tell the `sofia` profile to `rescan` or `reload`.

The `reload` option will completely stop the `sofia` profile, dropping all calls in progress, and then restart the profile with the new changes applied. The `rescan` option is much less intrusive. Instead of stopping the profile altogether it simply looks for the changes made in the XML configuration and selectively applies them. Changes to a gateway only require a `rescan`. However, changes made to the `sofia` profile parameters require a `reload`.

How it works...

In step 2, you defined a very basic gateway containing a gateway name, a server name, a username, and a password. In step 3, you added a condition that matched 10-digit numbers and bridged calls to such numbers using your new gateway.

Note that in the `bridge` application in step 3 you utilize what was captured in your regular expression (`$1`) to pass along the number that was dialed.

Step 4 and step 5 simply tell FreeSWITCH to load your new profile into memory and activate it.

There's more...

Connecting to a provider is usually just the first step in configuring outbound calls. The following sections provide additional information on how to make your FreeSWITCH gateways more effective.

Adding prefixes to dial strings

You can add prefixes to the `bridge` dial strings in multiple ways. In the simplest form, you might want to add a country or area code to the beginning of a number. In the example, if you modify the bridge string from `sofia/gateway/providerA/$1` to `sofia/gateway/providerA/+1$1`, your calls will now be completed with a prefix of +1 in front of the 10-digit number. This is commonly referred to as E.164 format.

Another common strategy is to add an account code or customer code to the beginning of a gateway. To do this, you can add a prefix that is based on a channel variable. In this scenario, let's say you have a customer with account code 38234 and a customer with account code 93289. Each customer makes calls from a specific IP address. You might have an XML dialplan that looks like this:

```
<extension name="check_customer_1">
  <condition field="network_addr" expression="^2\.3\.4\.5$">
    <action application="set" data="accountcode=38234"
            inline="true"/>
  </condition>
</extension>

<extension name="check_customer_">
  <condition field="network_addr" expression="9\.8\.7\.6$">
    <action application="set" data="accountcode=93289"
            inline="true"/>
  </condition>
</extension>

<extension name="dial-10-digit-numbers">
  <condition field="accountcode" expression="^.+$"/>
  <condition field="destination_number" expression="^(\d{10})$">
    <action application="bridge"
            data="sofia/gateway/providerA/${accountcode}$1"/>
  </condition>
</extension>
```

In the example, we first set the appropriate $accountcode variable (inline) during dialplan processing to identify the client. We then bridge to the provider only if the accountcode variable is set, and utilize the accountcode in the dial-string (see bold portion of bridge command)

Monitoring gateways

There are many additional parameters available on your gateway profile. One such parameter is the OPTIONS ping setting. This tells FreeSWITCH to ping the gateway periodically and ensure it's up. This is useful so that, if the gateway is down, you do not hang while trying to reach the gateway and can instead do error handling and/or move on to a new gateway/carrier.

To implement OPTIONS pings, simply add this parameter to your gateway definition (step 2 in *How to do it*):

```
<param name="ping" value="25"/>
```

This will ping the gateway every 25 seconds to ensure it's up. Note that at the time of this writing the lowest ping value allowed by FreeSWITCH is five seconds. If the gateway is down, FreeSWITCH will continue sending OPTIONS pings at the specified interval.

Configuring Google Voice

Google Voice (also known as Google Talk) is accessed via the mod_dingaling module, which provides XMPP support. (If you would like to learn more about XMPP, visit http://xmpp.org.) Mod_dingaling can act as both a XMPP server and a XMPP client, though it is generally used for its client abilities. With Google Voice, XMPP simply serves to establish sessions (much like SIP) and the audio properties and stream are otherwise merely RTP, just as in any VoIP call, using codecs you already know, like PCMU, GSM, and so on.

When using Google Voice with FreeSWITCH, your FreeSWITCH system initiates connections to or from Google Voice and can convert the audio and signaling into any other form—including SIP. This allows calls from Google Voice to your SIP phone and vice versa.

Getting ready

To get started, you're going to need your Google Voice user credentials. The process after that is straightforward.

How to do it...

You will need to modify the jingle profile's client file, which is located in conf/jingle_profiles/client.xml and then load (or reload) mod_dingaling.

1. Open client.xml in a text editor and change the highlighted lines:

```xml
<include>
  <profile type="gtalk">
    <param name="name" value="gmail.com"/>
    <param name="login" value="user@gmail.com/gtalk"/>
    <param name="password" value="your_password"/>
    <param name="dialplan" value="XML"/>
    <param name="context" value="public"/>
    <param name="exten" value="7901"/>
    <param name="rtp-ip" value="auto"/>
    <param name="auto-login" value="true"/>
    <param name="sasl" value="plain"/>
    <param name="server" value="talk.google.com"/>
    <param name="tls" value="true"/>
    <param name="use-rtp-timer" value="true"/>
    <param name="vad" value="both"/>
```

```
        <param name="local-network-acl" value="localnet.auto"/>
    </profile>
</include>
```

Change the values of the highlighted items in the code to your Google Talk/Google Voice username and password. Also, change the XML dialplan context and extension to route incoming calls to your desired destination.

2. Issue `reloadxml` at the CLI.

3. Make sure `mod_dingaling` is loaded in FreeSWITCH. At the CLI, type:

   load mod_dingaling

4. Add a way to make outbound calls via the new XMPP connection (this should look similar to your other gateways, as described earlier):

```
<extension name="dial-10-digit-numbers">
  <condition field="destination_number"
             expression="^(\d{10})$">
    <action application="bridge"
            data="dingaling/gtalk/+1$1@voice.google.com"/>
  </condition>
</extension>
```

How it works...

`mod_dingaling` controls messaging to/from Google Talk using XMPP. It uses profiles to define usernames, passwords, and servers with which to communicate. You can have as many profiles as you like, and each one is accessible with this dialstring syntax: `dingaling/PROFILE_NAME/destination@voice.google.com`.

In FreeSWITCH, XMPP profiles are called "jingle profiles".

Codec configuration

Codec configuration is very versatile in FreeSWITCH. In IP telephony, there are several differing scenarios for negotiating and choosing codecs. To meet the varying demands, FreeSWITCH has several configurable modes of operation as well as real-time variables that can influence how codec negotiation takes place. Typically the goal should be to reduce transcoding or resampling as much as possible. Transcoding is the case where two sides of the call have different codecs and audio flowing in either direction has to be completely decoded and re-encoded to the opposite channel's format. Resampling is similar but it is required when each side of the call is running at a different sample rate and the audio has to be "resampled" to the correct rate. One or both of these can be necessary depending on where you direct your calls to and how you have your codec configuration set.

Getting ready

The biggest decision to make up front is late-negotiation or early-negotiation. This setting tells FreeSWITCH to either validate the codec before the channel even hits the dialplan or to wait until the moment where media is absolutely necessary to perform codec negotiation. This gives you a chance to decide on a codec from your dialplan logic or even from the result of an outgoing call you intend to bridge. With early-negotiation, there is not much you can do to control the codec behavior of inbound calls so for this recipe we will work with late-negotiation. To prepare follow these steps:

1. Open your `sofia` profile `conf/sip_profiles/internal.xml` in a text editor and look for this line:

   ```
   <!--<param name="inbound-late-negotiation" value="true"/>-->
   ```

2. Uncomment this parameter to enable late-negotiation for all calls.

3. Save the file and exit. At the `fs_cli` press *F6* or issue the `reloadxml` command and then issue the command `sofia profile internal restart`.

You are now ready to experiment with codec negotiation.

How to do it...

To test late codec negotiation, follow these steps:

1. Add the following extension to your dialplan. Create `conf/dialplan/default/01_codec_negotiation.xml` and add these lines:

   ```
   <include>
     <extension name="example">
       <condition field="destination_number" expression="^1234$">
         <action application="set" data="inherit_codec=true"/>
         <action application="bridge"
                 data="sofia/internal/1234@cluecon.com"/>
       </condition>
     </extension>
   </include>
   ```

2. Save the file and exit. At `fs_cli`, issue the `reloadxml` command or press *F6*.

How it works...

Once the late-negotiation parameter is set you can set a special channel variable called `absolute_codec_string`. This variable is the same format as all other codec parameters inside FreeSWITCH and contains a comma separated list of codec names with modifiers to choose the rate or interval such as `G729`, `PCMU@30i`, or `speex@16000h`. The `@i` means to set the interval (milliseconds of audio per packet) and the `@h` sets the hertz (sampling rate) of the codec. So a simple dialplan that sets `absolute_codec_string`, then places an outbound call, can demonstrate how to choose a codec using late-negotiation:

```
<extension name="example">
  <condition field="destination_number" expression="^888$">
    <action application="set"
            data="absolute_codec_string=PCMU@30i"/>
    <action application="conference" data="888@default"/>
  </condition>
</extension>
```

Let's take it a step further. Say you are placing an outbound call to one or more servers and you want to avoid transcoding, but you don't know what codec that outbound call will offer and it would be too late at that point to set the `absolute_codec_string`. The solution is to use another important variable called `inherit_codec`. This variable, when set to `true`, tells FreeSWITCH to automatically set `absolute_codec_string` to the value of the codec that was negotiated by the outbound leg in the case of a bridged call. This way, you can allow the outbound call to negotiate a codec then pass that decided value back to the inbound leg before media was established. This will then force the inbound leg to request the same codec as the outbound leg and eliminate transcoding.

When calling the example extension, the call hits the XML dialplan and executes the instructions contained in the `action` tags. First, the variable `inherit_codec` is set to `true` and then the call is bridged to `1234@cluecon.com` over SIP. Because we enabled the `inbound-late-negotiation` parameter, the codec has not yet been chosen for the inbound leg. The outbound leg then proceeds to connect to `cluecon.com` where a codec will be chosen when the far-end answers or establishes media. At this point the FreeSWITCH call origination engine will take the codec from the outbound leg and set it as the `absolute_codec_string` on the inbound leg. Next, the media indication is passed across, which will prompt the inbound leg to negotiate media and offer the same codec as the outbound leg.

There's more...

You can also limit the codecs you offer to the outbound leg with another special variable called `ep_codec_string`. The `ep_codec_string` variable contains the list of codecs offered by the calling endpoint. This variable is the same one used by the `inherit_codec` behavior and can be used on an inbound call to make sure you only offer codecs on the outbound leg that were initially offered to the inbound leg. Here is the previous example with this extra functionality enabled:

```
<extension name="example">
  <condition field="destination_number" expression="^1234$">
    <action application="set" data="inherit_codec=true"/>
    <action application="export"
     data="nolocal:absolute_codec_string=${ep_codec_string}"/>
    <action application="bridge"
            data="sofia/internal/1234@cluecon.com"/>
  </condition>
</extension>
```

The `export` application sets the desired variable on the inbound leg, just like the `set` application, but marks it to be copied to (that is "exported" to) any outbound call legs generated by the channel on which it is set. The `nolocal:` syntax prevents the variable from applying to the channel on which it was set but still copies it to any outbound legs. So in this case we use `export` to set `nolocal:absolute_codec_string` to the current value of `ep_codec_string` for any outbound calls. This means when we bridge to `1234@cluecon.com` our `absolute_codec_string` will be set to exactly what codecs the inbound leg was offered.

Avoiding codec negotiation altogether

It's also possible to route your calls to a script or some other application that does not require media and uses logic to influence the `absolute_codec_string` in similar ways to what was demonstrated earlier. If you want to try to be completely uninvolved with the codec negotiation, you can try setting the variable `bypass_media` to `true` before you call the `bridge` application and FreeSWITCH will present the inbound SDP to the outbound leg and vice-versa, completely eliminating FreeSWITCH from the media path but still keeping it in the signaling path. This , however, does not work well under NAT conditions.

3
Processing Call Detail Records

In this chapter, we will cover:

- ► Using CSV CDRs
- ► Using XML CDRs
- ► Inserting CDRs into a backend database
- ► Using a web server to handle CDRs
- ► Using the event socket to handle CDRs

Introduction

Call detail records (**CDRs**) are an important part of the accounting process on any phone system. They are also an invaluable resource for troubleshooting. FreeSWITCH provides several different methods for generating CDRs. The most common method is to create plain-text, **comma-separated value** (**CSV**) files. Each line in the CSV file represents one phone call (or, more accurately, one call leg). There are other options for processing CDRs, most notably using mod_xml_cdr to store more detailed information about calls as well as using the event socket to process CDR information.

Using CSV CDRs

It is a simple matter to store CDRs in CSV format. This recipe describes the steps necessary to store call records in plain-text CSV files.

Getting ready

In the default configuration, `mod_cdr_csv` is compiled and enabled by default. CDR data is stored in the `$FS_INSTALL/log/cdr-csv/` directory. To review the options available, open the file `conf/autoload_configs/cdr_csv.conf.xml`. Here are the parameters available in the settings section:

```
<settings>
    <!-- 'cdr-csv' will always be appended to log-base -->
    <!--<param name="log-base" value="/var/log"/>-->
    <param name="default-template" value="example"/>
    <!-- This is like the info app but after the call is hung up -->
    <!--<param name="debug" value="true"/>-->
    <param name="rotate-on-hup" value="true"/>
    <!-- may be a b or ab -->
    <param name="legs" value="a"/>
    <!-- Only log in Master.csv -->
    <!-- <param name="master-file-only" value="true"/> -->
</settings>
```

We will review some of these options in the following section.

How to do it...

The easiest way to see a new CDR is to use a utility such as `cat` in Linux/Unix or `type` in Windows. Alternatively, if you are in a Linux/Unix environment you can use the `tail` utility to see the end of a text file (Windows does not ship with a `tail` utility, but there are free and open source options available).

Here are steps you can use in a Linux/Unix environment:

1. Change directory into `/usr/local/freeswitch/log/cdr-csv/`.
2. Execute `tail -f Master.csv` to display new CDR entries.
3. Make a test call, perhaps from one phone to another.
4. Hang up the test call and note the new CDR that is appended to `Master.csv`.
5. Press *Ctrl + C* to exit the `tail` command.

Here is a sample CDR from a call made from 1001 to 1007:

```
"Michael Collins","1001","1007","default","2011-03-02 12:09:25","2011-
03-02 12:09:26","2011-03-02 12:09:29","4","3","NORMAL_
CLEARING","f896639c-4508-11e0-a4cb-fb7d5a93c62e","f89d504e-4508-11e0-
a4cc-fb7d5a93c62e","1001","G722","G722"
```

How it works...

By watching the `Master.csv` file we can observe new CDRs being written to disk. While not particularly useful in a production system, doing this helps us to learn about CDRs and the information they contain. Furthermore, it is a simple troubleshooting tool you can use down the road.

There's more...

There are a number of things to keep in mind when using CSV CDRs. The following sections will help you make the best use of them.

File names and locations

If you do a directory listing of `log/cdr-csv` you will probably see a number of files in addition to `Master.csv`. For example, if you make a call from 1001 to 1007, you will see a file named `1001.csv` (note that, this file name is controlled by the user's `accountcode` parameter in their directory configuration). By default, each directory user has his/her own `.csv` file that contains only that user's call records. This is purely a feature for convenience and can be disabled in `conf/autoload_configs/cdr_csv.conf.xml` by setting this parameter:

```
<param name="master-file-only" value="true"/>
```

You may see other files with date/time stamps in their names like this:

```
Master.csv.2011-02-24-16-51-06
```

These files are created when a log rotate has been requested. This behavior can also be changed by setting this parameter:

```
<param name="rotate-on-hup" value="false"/>
```

Lastly, you can specify the base directory name where the `cdr-csv/` directory will be created and written to by using the `base-log` parameter. For example, setting `<param name="log-base" value="/var/log"/>` will force all CSV CDR files to be written to the `/var/log/cdr-csv/` directory.

> When changing parameters in `cdr_csv.conf.xml` be sure to save your changes and then issue the `reload mod_cdr_csv` command at the `fs_cli` in order for the changes to take effect.

Other options

There are a few other options in the settings section of `cdr_csv.conf.xml`. The first one is the debug parameter. Setting this to `true` will simply cause each call to perform an information dump (like the `info` dialplan application) when the call hangs up. Note that this will dump both to the `fs_cli` and to the FreeSWITCH log file, so be aware of disk space.

The other option is called `legs`. This will determine which call leg or legs get a CDR. By default only the A leg (that is the calling leg) gets a CDR. You can set this parameter to "b" to log only the B leg (that is the called leg) or you can set it to "ab" so that you receive a CDR for each leg. Handling A and B legs is discussed later in this chapter.

CDR CSV templates

The `default-template` parameter determines which CDR template is used when creating the CDR record. Notice the `<templates>` section of `cdr_csv.conf.xml`. There are various templates that you can use or edit. You may also create your own templates. By default we use the example template. Feel free to change or edit the `default-template` parameter to use a different template. The `asterisk` template will output CDRs in the format used by the Asterisk PBX. The `sql` template will output records in a particularly useful format which we will discuss in the recipe *Inserting CDRs into a backend database*.

Templates have another feature that allows for custom behavior. When a channel has the variable `accountcode` set to the name of a template, that call's CDR will be formatted in the specified template. You can test this behavior by editing a directory user and setting his or her account code:

1. Open `conf/directory/default/1007.xml` and set this value:

    ```
    <variable name="accountcode" value="sql"/>
    ```

2. Save the file and exit. Issue `reloadxml` at `fs_cli`.

3. Make a test call from 1007 to another phone, answer, then hangup.

4. You will now have a file named `sql.csv` in your `cdr-csv/` directory.

This technique can be used to customize the kinds of data that are stored. For example, you may have a client whose records need to have custom channel variables included in the CDR file, however you may not want every call in your system to include that information. Using `accountcode` and a CDR CSV template allows you to tailor the behavior as needed.

See also

▶ Refer to the *Inserting CDRs into a backend database* recipe later in this chapter

Using XML CDRs

XML CDRs have a wealth of information that cannot be easily represented in a traditional CSV flat-file format. In this recipe, we will enable `mod_xml_cdr` and discuss a few of its configuration options.

Getting ready

In the default configuration, `mod_xml_cdr` is compiled but is not enabled. Follow these steps to enable it:

1. Open `conf/autoload_configs/modules.conf.xml`.
2. Uncomment this line:

   ```
   <!-- <load module="mod_xml_cdr"/> -->
   ```

3. Save the file and exit.

Now `mod_xml_cdr` will load automatically when FreeSWITCH starts. However, if FreeSWITCH is already running then we need to load it manually. Simply issue the command `load mod_xml_cdr` at the `fs_cli` and the module will be loaded. XML CDR data will now be stored in the `$FS_INSTALL/log/xml-cdr/` directory.

XML CDRs have many options. To review them, open the file `conf/autoload_configs/xml_cdr.conf.xml`. We will be discussing some of these options later in this recipe.

How to do it...

The easiest way to see a new XML CDR is to use a utility like `cat` in Linux/Unix or `type` in Windows (note that, the Windows Powershell has an alias for the `cat` command). Alternatively you can use a utility such as `less` to page through the contents of a file. Both Windows and Linux/Unix support piping the output to `more` to achieve the same effect.

Here are steps you can use in a Linux/Unix environment:

1. Change directory into `/usr/local/freeswitch/log/xml-cdr/`.
2. List the directory contents with the `ls` command.
3. Make a test call, perhaps from one phone to another.
4. Hang up the test call and note the new XML CDR named `a_uuid.xml`.
5. Type `less a_uuid.xml` and press *Enter* to see the contents of the XML CDR file.

How it works...

By watching the `log/xml-cdr/` directory we can observe new CDRs being written to the disk. While not particularly useful in a production system, doing this helps us learn about XML CDRs and the information they contain. Furthermore, it is a simple troubleshooting tool you can use in the future.

What is a UUID?

When dealing with CDRs, and especially XML CDRs, you will be presented with many UUIDs. **UUID** stands for **Universally Unique Identifier.** It is a string of 32 hexadecimal digits divided into five groups, separated by hyphens. An example UUID is `678a195f-8431-4d77-8f10-550f7435f18e`. Each call leg receives a UUID in order to keep it distinct from all other call legs.

There's more...

The `mod_xml_cdr` module can do many things, not the least of which is to post new XML CDR information to a web server. The web server can then process the XML CDR, whether that means simply updating a database or performing other billing functions. These are discussed further in the recipe *Using a web server to handle CDRs* later in this chapter.

File names and locations

In the `conf/autoload_configs/xml_cdr.conf.xml` file there are two parameters in the `<settings>` section that affect file names and locations. The first parameter is called `prefix-a-leg`. When set to `true`, the A leg XML CDRs will have "a_" prefixed to the file name. This makes it easier to distinguish between A leg and B leg files.

The other parameter is `log-dir`. When set to an absolute path it will change the location where `/xml-cdr/` is located. For example:

```
<param name="log-dir" value="/var/log"/>
```

This will cause all XML CDRs to be written to the `/var/log/xml-cdr/` directory (you can also set it to a relative path, but that is rarely used).

Note: when changing parameters in `xml_cdr.conf.xml` be sure to save your changes and then issue the `reload mod_xml_cdr` command at the `fs_cli` in order for the changes to take effect.

Logging the B leg

By default, `mod_xml_cdr` only logs the A leg (that is the calling leg) of the call. If you wish to log the B leg (that is the called leg) then set this parameter:

```
<param name="log-b-leg" value="true"/>
```

This will cause B leg XML CDRs to be written. Note that B leg CDRs will always be named `uuid.xml` where `uuid` is the actual UUID of the call. There is no option to prefix the file name with "b_" like there is with the A leg.

See also

▶ Refer to the *Using a web server to handle CDRs* recipe later in this chapter

Inserting CDRs into a backend database

Frequently it is necessary to put CDR information into a database such as MySQL, PostgreSQL, or other SQL databases. FreeSWITCH does not support writing CDRs directly to a database (the decision not to write directly to a database is an engineering, not a technical limitation). This recipe discusses the simple method of writing SQL-based CSV files and then using those to update a backend database.

Getting ready

Of course, you will need a database in which to store your files. Any SQL-compliant database will work as long as you can use the command line to execute SQL statements. Create a database for your CDRs and allow any necessary access. This is completely dependent upon the type of database you have—consult your database documentation for specific instructions.

You will also need a table for the CDRs. The following CREATE TABLE syntax for a PostgreSQL database will work for the existing `sql` template in `cdr_csv.conf.xml`:

```
CREATE TABLE cdr (
    caller_id_name character varying(30),
    caller_id_number character varying(30),
    destination_number character varying(30),
    context character varying(20),
    start_stamp timestamp without time zone,
    answer_stamp timestamp without time zone,
    end_stamp timestamp without time zone,
    duration integer,
    billsec integer,
    hangup_cause character varying(50),
    uuid uuid,
```

```
    bleg_uuid uuid,
    accountcode character varying(10),
    read_codec character varying(20),
    write_codec character varying(20)
);
```

A similar CREATE TABLE command works for MySQL as follows:

```
CREATE TABLE cdr (
    caller_id_name varchar(30) DEFAULT NULL,
    caller_id_number varchar(30) DEFAULT NULL,
    destination_number varchar(30) DEFAULT NULL,
    context varchar(20) DEFAULT NULL,
    start_stamp datetime DEFAULT NULL,
    answer_stamp datetime DEFAULT NULL,
    end_stamp datetime DEFAULT NULL,
    duration int(11) DEFAULT NULL,
    billsec int(11) DEFAULT NULL,
    hangup_cause varchar(50) DEFAULT NULL,
    uuid varchar(100) DEFAULT NULL,
    bleg_uuid varchar(100) DEFAULT NULL,
    accountcode varchar(10) DEFAULT NULL,
    domain_name varchar(100) DEFAULT NULL
);
```

All the examples in this recipe will use a database name of "cdr" and a table name of "cdr". The last thing to do is to set the `sql` template as the default CDR template. Follow these steps:

1. Open `conf/autoload_configs/cdr_csv.conf.xml`.

2. Change the default-template parameter to `<param name="default-template" value="sql"/>`.

3. Save the file and exit. Issue the `reload mod_cdr_csv` command at the `fs_cli`.

4. Issue the `fsctl send_sighup` command at the `fs_cli` to rotate the log files.

You are now ready to create and process CDRs.

How to do it...

Follow these steps to get a call record into your new database table:

1. Make a test call from one phone to another, answer, wait a moment, and then hang up (you should now have at least one record in `Master.csv`).

2. Issue the `fsctl send_sighup` command at the `fs_cli`.

3. List the contents of your `log/cdr-csv/` directory and note the presence of a rotated `Master.csv` file, for example `Master.csv.2011-03-02-16-25-21`.

4. The rotated `Master.csv` file is the one to use for inserting records into your database. You will need to use your specific database's command line client to insert the records. For PostgreSQL use a command like this:

```
cat Master.csv.2011-03-02-16-44-29 | tr \" \' | psql -U postgres
cdr
```

5. Confirm the presence of the record in the cdr table with a simple SQL query like `SELECT * FROM cdr`. Delete the rotated `Master.csv` file.

How it works...

The `mod_cdr_csv sql` template writes out CDRs in the format of a single SQL `INSERT` statement per line. A sample record looks like this:

```
INSERT INTO cdr VALUES ("Michael Collins","1001","1007","defa
ult","2011-03-02 17:02:21","2011-03-02 17:02:23","2011-03-02
17:02:25","4","2","NORMAL_CLEARING","e4cfe0b2-4531-11e0-b634-
d7bcff4e7b8a","e4d6b072-4531-11e0-b635-d7bcff4e7b8a", "1001");
```

These `INSERT` statements can be piped into a database's command line client. Note the use of `tr` to translate double quotes to single quotes for compatibility with PostgreSQL.

 Your production environment may have specific requirements when it comes to things like single versus double quotes in PostgreSQL. Using the Unix `tr` command is one method of handling the issue. You could also modify the template to use single quotes instead of double quotes.

Finally, after confirming that the CDR was successfully inserted into the database we deleted the rotated file. We could also archive those to another disk volume as a backup.

There's more...

Most system administrators will recognize that the commands presented here are easily scriptable. Indeed, this is one reason why the FreeSWITCH developers did not create a native direct-to-database module for CDRs. It is much safer to write CDRs directly to disk and then have a `cron` job (or something similar) to perform all of the tasks. By breaking them down into discrete tasks, rather than abstracting them away in a FreeSWITCH module, it becomes easier to create robust, scalable solutions using proven methods.

In fact, you could set up a CDR database on a completely separate machine, and use basic tools like `fs_cli` to rotate logs and `scp` or `ftp` to pull the files over to the local database server. An intelligent script could then notify the system administrator of any issues. Also, as long as there is disk space on the FreeSWITCH server, no CDR records will be lost in case of a failed connection between the CDR server and the FreeSWITCH server. CDRs will continue to be written to disk on the FreeSWITCH server and can be collected and processed when connectivity has been re-established.

See also

▶ Refer to the *Getting familiar with the "fs_cli" interface* recipe in *Chapter 4*

Using a web server to handle XML CDRs

One feature of FreeSWITCH's `mod_xml_cdr` is that it can use `HTTP POST` actions to send CDR data to a web server which in turn can process those, perhaps putting them into a database. This mechanism has several advantages:

▶ Modern web servers can handle enormous amounts of traffic

▶ Multiple FreeSWITCH servers can post to a single CDR Server

▶ Multiple web servers can be set up to allow failover and redundancy

The recipe presented here will focus on the steps needed to get a web server set up to process incoming POST requests with XML CDR data.

Getting ready

You will need an operational web server that you control. Most Linux/Unix and Windows systems can have an Apache web server installed. Detailed instructions on configuring a web server are beyond the scope of this book, however such instructions are available in numerous books and on the Internet. This recipe will assume a clean install of the Apache web server, but the principles apply to other servers such as Lighttpd and Nginx. For this example we will assume the Apache server is on the same machine as your FreeSWITCH install.

How to do it...

Enable `mod_xml_cdr` on your server. (Refer to the *Using XML CDRs* recipe earlier in this chapter). Next, follow these steps:

1. Open `conf/autoload_configs/xml_cdr.conf.xml` and locate this line:

```
<!-- <param name="url"
            value="http://localhost/cdr_curl/post.php"/> -->
```

2. Change the line to this:

```
<param name="url" value="http://localhost/cgi-bin/cdr.pl"/>
```

3. Save the file and exit.

4. In your system's cgi-bin directory, create a new file named cdr.pl (the cgi-bin directory is usually /usr/lib/cgi-bin but may be different on older systems). Add these lines to the file:

```
#!/usr/bin/perl
  use strict;
  use warnings;
  use CGI;
  $|++;
    my $q = CGI->new;
    my $raw_cdr = $q->param('cdr');
    open (FILEOUT,'>','/tmp/cdr.txt');
    print FILEOUT $raw_cdr;
  close(FILEOUT);
print $q->header();
```

5. Save the file and exit.

6. Make the file executable with this command:

chmod +x /usr/lib/cgi-bin/cdr.pl

7. Log in to fs_cli and press *F6* or issue the reloadxml command.

8. Make a test call and you should see the XML CDR contents in the /tmp/cdr.txt file.

How it works...

This is a simple Perl-based CGI script. All it does is pull the cdr parameter out of the POST data that is submitted by mod_xml_curl. Once it has this value (in the variable $raw_cdr) it dumps the CDR into the temporary file named /tmp/cdr.txt.

While this example is not particularly useful for production, it demonstrates the minimal steps required to get the POSTed CDR data into the system. If you are more comfortable with another scripting language, such as PHP, Python, or Ruby, you may just as easily process the CDRs with those languages. Here is a simple version in PHP:

```
$raw_cdr = $_POST['cdr'];
  $writefile = fopen('/tmp/dump.txt',"w");
  fwrite($writefile, $raw_cdr);
fclose($writefile);
```

Once you have the data in your program you have more options for processing it.

There's more...

A common practice with handling XML CDR data with a CGI script (or Fast CGI or some other appropriate method to handle an HTTP POST request) is to process the data and then put it into a database. This section describes how to insert the CDR into the same database table that we created in the previous *Inserting CDRs into a backend database* recipe.

Assuming you have a database named "cdr" with a table also named "cdr", you can use this modified `cdr.pl` script to insert the records right into the database.

 You will need to use the `cpan` tool to install the `DBI` module and the `DBD` driver for your database. Common ones are `DBD::mysql` and `DBD::PgPP`. This example assumes `DBD::PgPP`, the Postgres "pure perl" database driver.

The modified `cdr.pl` is as follows:

```perl
#!/usr/bin/perl
use strict;
use warnings;
use CGI;
use DBI;
use Data::Dump qw(dump);
$|++;
  my $q = CGI->new;
  my $raw_cdr = $q->param('cdr');
  my @all_fields = qw(caller_id_name caller_id_number
  destination_number context start_stamp answer_stamp end_stamp
  duration billsec hangup_cause uuid bleg_uuid \
  accountcode read_codec write_codec);
    my @fields;
    my @values;
    foreach my $field (@all_fields) {
      next unless $raw_cdr =~ m/$field>(.*?)</;
      push @fields, $field;
      push @values, "'" . urldecode($1) . "'";
    }
    my $cdr_line;
    my $query = sprintf(
    "INSERT INTO %s (%s) VALUES (%s);",
    'cdr', join(',', @fields), join(',', @values)
    );
  my $db = DBI->connect('DBI:PgPP:dbname=cdr;host=localhost',
  'postgres', 'postgres');
```

```
    $db->do($query);
print $q->header();
sub urldecode {
  my $url = shift;
  $url =~ s/%([a-fA-F0-9]{2,2})/chr(hex($1))/eg;
  return $url;
}
```

This script is a simple example of inserting records into the database. The @all_
fields array is a list of every field in the cdr table. We cycle through this list looking for
corresponding values. If we find one, we use urldecode and then add the field name to the
@fields list and its value goes into @values. From there we create a query string using the
@fields and @values arrays and then insert them into the database.

See also

▸ Refer to the *Using XML CDRs* and *Inserting records into a backend database* recipes
  from earlier in this chapter

Using the event socket to handle CDRs

Sometimes you need to get CDR information immediately. FreeSWITCH accommodates those
needs with the powerful event socket. This recipe will briefly describe how to receive CDR
information on the event socket. You will also find more useful information on the event socket
interface in the following chapter.

Getting ready

This recipe relies on the event socket interface to FreeSWITCH. However, there are many
different ways of connecting to the event socket. Because of this we will use a simple
Perl script with the **event socket library (ESL)** to demonstrate the principles involved. Any
language that supports ESL can use the techniques demonstrated here.

Follow the steps in the *Setting up the event socket library* recipe found in *Chapter 4*.
Specifically, build the Perl module in order to run the example script.

How to do it...

Enter this script (or download it from the Packt website at http://www.packtpub.com):

```perl
#!/usr/bin/perl
# handle_cdr.pl
# Connect to event socket, listen for CHANNEL_HANGUP_COMPLETE events
# Uses event data to create custom CDRs
  use strict;
```

```perl
use warnings;
use lib '/usr/src/freeswitch.git/libs/esl/perl';
use ESL;
   my $host = "localhost";
   my $port = "8021";
   my $pass = "ClueCon";
   my $con  = new ESL::ESLconnection($host, $port, $pass);
     if ( ! $con ) {
        die "Unable to establish connection to FreeSWITCH.\n";
     }
## Listen for events, filter in only CHANNEL_HANGUP_COMPLETE
   $con->events('plain','all');
   $con->filter('Event-Name','CHANNEL_HANGUP_COMPLETE');
     print "Connected to FreeSWITCH $host:$port and waiting for
     events...\n\n";
     while (1) {
       my @raw_data = split "\n",$e->serialize();
       my %cdr;
       foreach my $item ( @raw_data ) {
         #print "$item\n";
         my ($header, $value) = split ': ', $item;
         $header =~ s/^variable_//;
         $cdr{$header} = $value;
       }
       # %cdr contains a complete list of channel variables
       print "New CDR: ";
       print $cdr{uuid} . ', ' . $cdr{direction} . ', ';
       print $cdr{answer_epoch} . ', ' . $cdr{end_epoch} . ', ';
       print $cdr{hangup_cause} . "\n";
     }
```

Run this script and make a test call. An abbreviated CDR will be printed to the screen. Press
Ctrl + C to exit the script.

How it works...

The basic principles involved are as follows:

   ▶   Establish an ESL connection to FreeSWITCH

   ▶   Subscribe to CHANNEL_HANGUP_COMPLETE events by using a filter

   ▶   Process each event as an individual CDR

If you are more familiar with PHP, Python, or Ruby you should be able to translate these
concepts from our demonstration script.

There's more...

Here are a few tips to help you make the most of using the event socket for CDRs.

ESL considerations

Keep in mind that the script will need to be able to find the ESL library. Note this line:

```
use lib '/usr/src/freeswitch.git/libs/esl/perl';
```

This tells Perl to look in the specified directory when using additional modules. Without it, the use of ESL directive would fail (alternatively you can install the requisite ESL files into your system's `site_perl` directory).

Another important point is that this method will receive two events for a normal call. The A leg and the B leg each generate a `CHANNEL_HANGUP_COMPLETE` event. The value in `$cdr{direction}` will be "inbound" for the A leg and will be "outbound" for the B leg.

Lastly, keep in mind that this line is blocking:

```
my $e = $con->recvEvent();
```

It will block the entire script until a new event arrives. See the *Filtering events* recipe in *Chapter 4* to see an example of the `recvEventTimed()` method that does not block.

Receiving XML CDRs

It is possible to receive the CDRs over the event socket in XML format. This is controlled on a per-call basis using the `hangup_complete_with_xml` channel variable. Set this variable to true in your dialplan as follows:

```
<action application="set" data=" hangup_complete_with_xml=true"/>
```

See also

▸   Refer to the *Using XML CDRs* recipe in this chapter for more information on XML-based CDRs

▸   Refer to the *Setting up the event socket library* and *Filtering events* recipes in *Chapter 4*

4
External Control

In this chapter, we will cover:

- ▶ Getting familiar with the `fs_cli` interface
- ▶ Setting up the event socket library
- ▶ Establishing an inbound event socket connection
- ▶ Establishing an outbound event socket connection
- ▶ Using `fs_ivrd` to manage outbound connections
- ▶ Filtering events
- ▶ Launching a call with an inbound event socket connection
- ▶ Using the ESL connection object for call control
- ▶ Using the built-in web interface

Introduction

One of the most powerful features of FreeSWITCH is the ability to connect to it and control it from an external resource. This is made possible by the powerful FreeSWITCH event system and its connection to the outside world: the event socket. The event socket interface is a simple TCP-based connection that programmers can use to connect to the inner-workings of a FreeSWITCH server. Furthermore, the FreeSWITCH developers have also created the **Event Socket Library** (**ESL**), which is an abstraction layer to make programming with the event socket a lot simpler. The following languages are supported by ESL:

- ▶ C/C++
- ▶ Lua
- ▶ Perl
- ▶ PHP
- ▶ Python

- ▶ Ruby
- ▶ TCL

Keep in mind that the ESL is only an abstraction library—you can connect to the event socket with any socket-capable application, including `telnet`!

The tips in this chapter will focus most of their attention on using the event socket for some common use cases. The last tip, though, will introduce a particularly interesting way to connect to FreeSWITCH externally without using the event socket, namely, using the built-in web server that is enabled when you install `mod_xml_rpc`. Regardless of how you wish to control FreeSWITCH, it is highly recommended that you read the first recipe in this chapter, *Getting familiar with the fs_cli interface*, as this will serve you well in all aspects of working with FreeSWITCH.

Getting familiar with the fs_cli interface

The preferred method of connecting to the FreeSWITCH console is to use the `fs_cli` program, where "fs_cli" stands for **FreeSWITCH Command-line Interface**. This program comes with FreeSWITCH, as part of the default installation, and works in Linux/Unix, Mac OS X, and Windows. What is less well known about `fs_cli` is that it is an excellent example of an ESL program. Beyond that, anything that you can do with `fs_cli`, you can do with ESL and the event socket. (Keep in mind that when you are logged in to `fs_cli` you can do *anything* that you can do at the FreeSWITCH console, including shutting down the system and disconnecting any calls. Exercise appropriate caution when using `fs_cli`.)

The natural first step in mastering the external control of FreeSWITCH is to become familiar with `fs_cli`. Indeed, it is one of the most important tools for interacting with your FreeSWITCH server.

 If you're familiar with C programming then you might appreciate the source code for `fs_cli`. It is found in `libs/esl/fs_cli.c` under the FreeSWITCH source directory.

Getting ready

The only prerequisites for running `fs_cli` are access to your system's command line and a running FreeSWITCH server with `mod_event_socket` enabled (on a default installation `mod_event_socket` is always enabled). However, you may find it convenient to allow `fs_cli` to be launched from any directory on your system. In a Linux/Unix environment you can add a symbolic link like this:

```
ln -s /usr/local/freeswitch/bin/fs_cli /usr/local/bin/fs_cli
```

Windows users can add the FreeSWITCH binary directory to their system's PATH variable.

How to do it...

Follow these steps:

1. Launch `fs_cli` by typing `fs_cli` (or in Windows, `fs_cli.exe`) and pressing *Enter*. A simple welcome screen will appear:

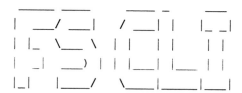

```
****************************************************
* Anthony Minessale II, Ken Rice, Michael Jerris   *
* FreeSWITCH (http://www.freeswitch.org)           *
* Paypal Donations Appreciated: paypal@freeswitch.org *
* Brought to you by ClueCon http://www.cluecon.com/  *
****************************************************


Type /help <enter> to see a list of commands


+OK log level   [7]
freeswitch@internal>
```

At this point you are at the `fs_cli` and can issue commands.

2. Try a simple command; type `/help` and press *Enter* and you will see a number of commands you can enter. All commands that begin with a forward slash (/) are specific to the `fs_cli` program.

3. You can also issue FreeSWITCH API commands. Type `show api` and press *Enter*. You will see quite a long list of FreeSWITCH API commands that are available.

4. Lastly, type `status` and press *Enter* to see a brief status report on your FreeSWITCH server.

How it works...

The `fs_cli` emulates the behavior of the FreeSWITCH console, which is available when FreeSWITCH is run in the foreground, that is, without the −nc flag ("nc" stands for "no console"). However, technically speaking, `fs_cli` is merely an event socket program. Everything sent and received with `fs_cli` is done over the FreeSWITCH event socket. Therefore, just about everything you can do from `fs_cli` you can also do with an event socket-based program. Keep in mind that the "slash" commands are specific to `fs_cli` and don't necessarily have an event socket equivalent, such as /help and /exit.

There are numerous ways to exit the `fs_cli` program. There are three "slash" commands, namely, /exit, /quit, and /bye. You can also type in three periods (. . .) and press *Enter*. On some systems you can press *Ctrl + D*.

There's more...

Now that you are familiar with the general usage of `fs_cli` it is good to learn about some of the more useful commands.

Important commands for listing information

FreeSWITCH administration frequently means getting information out of the server. Here is a list and brief description of some commands you will no doubt want to use. Feel free to try any of these on your system—they won't "break" anything—they simply give you information.

Command	Shortcut Key	Description
`sofia status`	F5	Display general SIP information
`sofia status profile internal`	F9	Display SIP information about the "internal" profile
`help`	F1	List available commands (equivalent to show api)
`show channels`	F3	List individual call legs
`show calls`	F4	List bridged calls
`/log 6`	None	Set log level to INFO (prevents the numerous "debug" messages from being displayed)
`/log 7`	F8	Set log level to DEBUG (all "debug" messages are displayed)

Useful command line options

The `fs_cli` program has a number of command-line options. You can view them all by executing `fs_cli -h` (or `fs_cli.exe -h` in Windows). The following are descriptions of some of the more useful options:

Option	Description
`-x`	Execute a command, then exit
`-r`	Retry connection (useful if you have just restarted FreeSWITCH and are reconnecting)
`-H`	Specify FreeSWITCH server host name or IP address to connect to
`-P`	Specify FreeSWITCH server port to connect to

The `-x` option is particularly useful for doing things from the command line. For example, try this command from your system's command prompt:

```
fs_cli -x "show channels"
```

You will receive the output from the show channels command and then be back at the command shell. This technique can be used in shell scripts.

> See the online documentation for `fs_cli` at `http://wiki.freeswitch.org/wiki/Fs_cli`. It includes descriptions of all the `fs_cli` commands as well as the handy `.fs_cli_conf` configuration file.

Viewing events

Event-based programming can be a daunting challenge at first. As a brief introduction it is good just to look at the events that come over the event socket. The `fs_cli` can do this very easily. At the `fs_cli` enter these two commands:

```
/log 0
```
```
/event plain all
```

Watch your screen for a few seconds and you will eventually see some events come in. Any time a call is handled on the system there will be numerous events. There are events for changes in call state, as well as new calls being set up and existing calls being torn down. Issue the `/noevents` command to stop seeing the events come through.

The rest of this chapter contains a great deal of information about event socket programming.

See also

▶   Refer to the *Filtering events* recipe in *Chapter 4*

Setting up the event socket library

Most event socket programming is not usually done in C, but rather one of the common scripting languages, like Perl, PHP, Python, and Ruby. The Event Socket Library (ESL) is available as a tool for those working in a Linux/Unix environment.

Getting ready

The most difficult part about using ESL with a scripting language is making sure that the necessary development libraries have been installed. This process varies among operating systems and languages. The instructions presented here are for Debian or Red Hat Linux variants. If your operating system is not among these then it is recommended that you check with the website for your language and look for instructions on how to install the development libraries.

Debian

Debian variants (such as Ubuntu) generally use the `apt` package manager. The development libraries can be installed with these commands:

```
apt-get install libperl-dev
apt-get install python-dev
apt-get install php5-dev
apt-get install ruby-dev
```

Red Hat

Red Hat Linux variants (RHEL, CentOS, Fedora) generally use the `yum` package manager. The development libraries can be installed with these commands:

```
yum install python-devel
yum install php-devel
yum install ruby-devel
```

Most Red Hat variants have the requisite Perl development files already installed.

How to do it...

Once you have the necessary library files installed for your language of choice then you are ready to do the actual build of ESL. Open a terminal and change directory into your FreeSWITCH source directory. From there execute these commands:

```
cd libs/esl
make
```

This will confirm that your system's ESL libraries are ready to be used. From here you can install the library for you language of choice. In our example we'll use Perl. Execute this command:

```
make perlmod-install
```

You can also do other languages using one of the following commands:

- make phpmod-install
- make pymod-install
- make rubymod (no -install here)

Once the installation is complete you can start using the ESL in your scripts.

How it works...

The make install commands will compile the ESL for each language and then install the necessary files into the language's include path. If you have a non-standard installation then you may have to install these files yourself. Once the files are installed you can use one of the test scripts for your language. For example, you can change directory to the perl/ subdirectory and run the single_command.pl script for testing:

```
cd perl
perl single_command.pl status
```

The other languages have sample scripts as well. Run a sample script to confirm that your ESL is working. From here you can move on to do other ESL-related tasks.

 If you get an error, such as **Can't call method "getBody" on an undefined value** then most likely FreeSWITCH is not running. Make sure FreeSWITCH is running, and also make sure that you can connect to it by using fs_cli.

Establishing an inbound event socket connection

An "inbound" event socket connection means that an external script or program is connecting to a FreeSWITCH server. The connection is inbound from the server's point of view. In fact, every time you run the fs_cli utility you are making an inbound event socket connection.

Getting ready

Be sure that you have installed ESL for your preferred programming language. (See the previous recipe, *Setting up the event socket library*.) From there you will just need a text editor, command-line access, and a phone registered to your system. The examples presented here are in Perl, however the accompanying code samples have corresponding examples in Python as well.

How to do it...

The following code is a simple inbound connection that sends the `status` command to FreeSWITCH. Add the code as follows:

1. Open `scripts/ib_api.pl` in a text editor and add these lines:

```perl
#!/usr/bin/perl
use strict;
use warnings;
require ESL;

my $host = "localhost";
my $port = "8021";
my $pass = "ClueCon";
my $con  = new ESL::ESLconnection($host, $port, $pass);
if (! $con) {
    die "Unable to establish connection to $host:$port\n";
}
my $cmd  = "status";
my $args = "";
my $e    = $con->api($cmd, $args);

if ( $e ) {
    print "Result of $cmd $args command:\n\n";
    print $e->getBody();
} else {
    die "No response to $cmd command.\n";
}
```

2. Save the file and exit.

3. Linux/Unix users can make the script executable with this command:

```
chmod +x ib_api.pl
```

4. Run the script and you will see the output of the `status` command.

Linux/Unix: `./ib_api.pl`

Windows: `perl.exe ib_api.pl`

How it works...

The script basically does these four things:

- ▸ Uses (that is, "requires") the ESL library
- ▸ Connects to FreeSWITCH with the `ESL::ESLconnection` object
- ▸ Issues the `status` command with the connection object's `api()` method
- ▸ Prints the results with the event object's `getBody()` method

Change the `$cmd` and `$args` values to issue a different command. For example, to see the results of "sofia status profile internal" you would set the variables like this:

```
my $cmd  = "sofia";
my $args = "status profile internal";
```

Note that we also do some very basic error checking. First, we confirm that we get a valid `ESL::ESLconnection` object. Second, we make sure that we receive an event object as a result of the `$con->api` call.

There's more...

The ESL event object has a number of methods. One of the most important ones is the `getBody()` method. However, not all events actually have a body—they simply have a list of headers. To see what the event headers look like, use the `serialize()` method like this:

```
print $e->serialize();
```

This will print out a list of headers and their corresponding values. (Try it!) You can also get an individual header value with the `getHeader()` method:

```
print $e->getHeader('Event-Name');
```

Keep in mind that we are using the `api()` method which blocks (that is, it waits for a response). This keeps things simple, however, there are times when blocking is not desired. The `ESL::ESLconnection` object also has a `bgapi()` method for executing API commands in a non-blocking manner. The `bgapi()` method is discussed further in the *Launch a call with inbound event socket connection* recipe later in this chapter.

See also

▶ Refer to the *Setting up the event socket library* and *Launching a call with inbound event socket connection* recipes in this chapter

Establishing an outbound event socket connection

An "outbound" event socket connection lets you control a call leg from a program that sits and waits for a TCP connection on a specific port. The dialplan `socket` application sends control of the call to the process listening on the specified TCP port. This recipe will guide you through the steps necessary to get a simple call control script up and running. You may find it easier to understand the information presented here if you are at least somewhat familiar with the concept of TCP sockets.

Getting ready

You will need a text editor and a telephone connected to FreeSWITCH as well as access to the `fs_cli` for your system. You will also need to have the ESL compiled and working for your scripting language of choice (see *Setting up the event socket Library (ESL)* earlier in this chapter). The language used in this is example is Perl, however the principles apply to all ESL-enabled languages. When we are through we will have a simple script that will listen for a socket connection from FreeSWITCH, answer the call, play a file, wait for a DTMF digit, and then exit.

How to do it...

Start by creating an extension for us to dial:

1. Open `conf/dialplan/default/01_Custom.xml` in a text editor and add this simple extension:

    ```
    <extension name="outbound event socket">
      <condition field="destination_number" data="^(5004)$">
        <action application="socket" data="127.0.0.1:8040"/>
      </condition>
    </extension>
    ```

2. Save the file and exit. Issue the `reloadxml` command or press *F6* at the `fs_cli`.

Now create the script:

1. Create the file `scripts/outbound_socket.pl` in a text editor and add these lines:

```perl
#!/usr/bin/perl
require ESL;
use IO::Socket::INET;

my $ip = "127.0.0.1";
my $sock = new IO::Socket::INET ( LocalHost => $ip,
                                  LocalPort => '8040',
                                  Proto => 'tcp',
                                  Listen => 1,
                                  Reuse => 1 );
die "Could not create socket: $!\n" unless $sock;

for(;;) {
    my $new_sock = $sock->accept();
    my $pid = fork();
    if ($pid) {
        print "New child pid $pid created...\n";
        close($new_sock);
        next;
    }

    my $fd = fileno($new_sock);
    my $con = new ESL::ESLconnection($fd);
    my $info = $con->getInfo();
    my $uuid = $info->getHeader("unique-id");

    printf "Connected call %s, from %s\n", $uuid,
            $info->getHeader("caller-caller-id-number");

    $con->sendRecv("myevents $uuid");
    $con->execute("answer");
    $con->execute("start_dtmf");
    $con->execute("playback",
                "ivr/ivr-welcome_to_freeswitch.wav");
    $con->execute("sleep","500");
    $con->execute("playback",
                "ivr/ivr-finished_pound_hash_key.wav");

    while($con->connected()) {
        my $e = $con->recvEvent();
        if ($e) {
            my $name = $e->getHeader("event-name");
```

```
                     print "EVENT [$name]\n";
                     if ($name eq "DTMF") {
                          my $digit = $e->getHeader("dtmf-digit");
                          my $duration = $e->getHeader("dtmf-duration");
                          print "DTMF digit $digit ($duration)\n";
                          $con->execute("hangup");
                     }
                }
           }
           print "BYE\n";
           close($new_sock);
      }
```

2. Save the file and exit.

3. Linux/Unix users make the script executable with this command:

   chmod +x outbound_socket.pl

4. Launch the script:

   Linux/Unix: `./outbound_socket.pl`

   Windows: `perl.exe outbound_socket.pl`

5. The script is now waiting for a connection. Dial *5004* from your phone and watch the script's output to see what it is doing.

How it works...

The script opens a "socket listener" on the local host IP address of 127.0.0.1 and TCP port 8040. When you call *5004*, it executes the `socket` application, which quite literally sends control of the call over to port 8040. The `socket` application has no idea what is listening on that port or even if there is anything listening (try dialing *5004* without the script running).

Once the socket connection is opened, the Perl script "forks" a "child process" and continues to listen for further connections (if we didn't do this then the script would exit after the first call it handled and we would need to restart it after each call). If the fork is successful then the new child process executes the code starting with this line:

```
    my $fd = fileno($new_sock);
```

Most of these lines are fairly obvious, but a few of them warrant some explanation. Let's start with these lines:

```
    my $fd  = fileno($new_sock);
    my $con = new ESL::ESLconnection($fd);
```

The $fd variable is a file descriptor for the socket connection that is opened. It is passed in to the new method of the ESL::ESLconnection object class to ensure that the $con object is communicating with the correct TCP stream from FreeSWITCH. Once we have the connection object ($con) we then get some information from it with these lines:

```
my $info = $con->getInfo();
my $uuid = $info->getHeader("unique-id");
```

The $info object is a representation of the initial burst of information that FreeSWITCH sends to the script when the socket connection is first established. The $uuid variable is populated with the call leg's UUID, which is found in the unique-id header of the $info object.

This line is important for outbound socket connections:

```
$con->sendRecv("myevents $uuid");
```

The myevents command is a special event socket directive that tells FreeSWITCH that this particular socket session will receive events only for this call leg. In effect, it filters out all FreeSWITCH events that do not pertain to this particular call leg. The sendRecv method sends an event socket command and waits for a response. Note that sendRecv is very different from the execute method. The execute method executes a dialplan application, whereas the sendRecv command sends an event socket command.

We use the execute method to play a few sound files and then we enter this important while loop:

```
while($con->connected()) {
    my $e = $con->recvEvent();
    if ($e) {
        ...
        }
    }
}
```

This control structure checks two things: the status of the connection and whether or not an event has been received. If the caller hangs up then $con->connected() will evaluate to false and the script will exit. Also, if the user presses a touch tone then the script will receive an event. The script is receiving other events as well, but we ignore anything that is not a DTMF key press.

Finally, if we receive an event then the $e object is populated and now we can check to see if it is a DTMF event:

```
my $name = $e->getHeader("event-name");
print "EVENT [$name]\n";
 if ($name eq "DTMF") {
```

For each event received we print out the name of the event, however, we only act upon receiving a DTMF event. We display some information about the DTMF that was received and then hang up the call.

There's more...

When the event socket connection is first made, FreeSWITCH sends an initial burst of information to the script. To see what this looks like, add this line right after the printf line:

```
print $info->serialize();
```

Make the call to *5004* again while watching the script's output. You will see that there is a tremendous amount of information that FreeSWITCH sends when the call is first established. Use the getHeader() method to retrieve a specific value from the $info object like we did with unique-id.

See also

- ▶ For an alternative way of handling multiple connections, see the *Using fs_ivrd to manage outbound connections* recipe in this chapter, which discusses a special utility to make the job easier
- ▶ Also refer to the *Setting up the event socket library* and *Using the ESL connection object for call control* recipes in this chapter

Using fs_ivrd to manage outbound connections

FreeSWITCH supplies a tool that offers a simplified means of creating interactive scripts. Unlike the socket application presented in *Using the ESL connection object for call control* in this chapter, using fs_ivrd relieves the programmer from having to maintain socket connections and handle child processes. The fs_ivrd tool provides a simple interface using the STDIN and STDOUT file handles. The example Perl script presented here uses the ESL::IVR Perl module supplied with ESL. As of this writing there had not been any other fs_ivrd modules written for any of the other scripting languages.

Getting ready

This example requires that the ESL Perl module be properly compiled. See *Setting up the event socket library* earlier in this chapter. Also, it is helpful to have at least two terminal windows open so that you can view the script as well as fs_cli. Note: fs_ivrd is not supported in Windows environments.

How to do it...

First, add a new extension to your dialplan by following these steps:

1. Edit or create a new file in `conf/dialplan/default/` named `01_event_socket.xml`.

2. Add this extension to the new file:

```
<extension name="fs_ivrd Example">
  <condition field="destination_number" expression="^(9950)$">
    <action application="log"
            data="INFO Starting fs_ivrd example..."/>
    <action application="set" data=
       "ivr_path=/usr/local/freeswitch/scripts/ivrd-example.pl"
     />
    <action application="socket" data="127.0.0.1:9090 full"/>
  </condition>
</extension>
```

3. Save the file, exit, then issue `reloadxml` or press *F6* at the `fs_cli` prompt.

This extension will call your `fs_ivrd` script when the user dials *9950*. Create the following script or download it from the Packt Publishing website:

1. Create a new file in `scripts/` called `ivrd-example.pl`.

2. Add the following lines:

```perl
#!/usr/bin/perl
use strict;
use warnings;
use ESL::IVR;

$| = 1;          # Turn off buffering
select STDERR; # Use this stream for console output
print "Starting ivrd-example.pl...\n\n";

my $con = new ESL::IVR;
my $uuid = $con->{_uuid};
my $dest = $con->getVar('destination_number');

$con->execute('answer');
$con->execute('sleep','500');
$con->playback('ivr/ivr-welcome_to_freeswitch.wav');
my $digits = "1";
my $prompt = 'file_string://voicemail/vm-to_exit.wav';
$prompt .= '!voicemail/vm-press.wav!digits/9.wav';
```

```perl
my $badinput = 'ivr/ivr-that_was_an_invalid_entry.wav';

while( $con->{_esl}->connected() ) {
   while ( $con->{_esl}->connected() && $digits != "9" ) {
      $con->playAndGetDigits(
            "1 1 3 5000 # $prompt $badinput mydigits \\d+");
      $digits = $con->getVar('mydigits');
      print "Received digit $digits\n";
      $con->playback("ivr/ivr-you_entered.wav");
      $con->execute("say","en number pronounced $digits");
      $con->execute("sleep","1000");
      if ( $digits == "9" ) {
         $con->playback('voicemail/vm-goodbye.wav');
      }
   }
   $con->execute("hangup");
}
```

3. Save the file and exit.

4. Make the file executable with this command:

   chmod +x ivrd-example.pl

5. Lastly, we need to launch the fs_ivrd daemon with this command:

   /usr/local/freeswitch/bin/fs_ivrd -h 127.0.0.1 -p 9090

6. Test the script by dialing 9950 and following the prompts.

How it works...

The fs_ivrd daemon runs constantly. In fact, you can run it in the background using whatever "bg" command is appropriate for your platform. When it receives a socket connection from FreeSWITCH it launches whatever script is specified in the ivr_path channel variable and handles all inter-process communications. The ivrd-example.pl script simply establishes an ESL connection using the ESL::IVR module. The resulting $con object is a superset of the standard ESL connection object.

Once the connection is made, the actual call control is quite simple: we answer the call, pause, then greet the caller. We then enter an outer while loop that detects whether or not the caller has hung up. The inner while loop checks for two conditions:

▸ Whether or not the caller hung up

▸ Whether the caller dialed 9

If either case is true then the script exits, otherwise we simply ask the caller to press a digit, read it back, and loop around again.

Building custom, interactive call control scripts with `ESL::IVR` is all but trivial. Simply use the `ivrd-example.pl` script as a template. Note that your script can also use any other Perl modules available on your system, such as the DBI module for database access.

See also

▸ The *Establishing an outbound event socket connection* and *Using the ESL connection object for call control* recipes in this chapter

Filtering events

Events are the lifeblood of the FreeSWITCH eventing system. FreeSWITCH throws events for virtually everything that happens. This can overwhelm a program (and indeed the programmer) with a flood of information. The solution is to use the FreeSWITCH event filter feature.

Getting ready

Learning about filters is very simple. Initially we will just use `fs_cli` connected to a FreeSWITCH server. Later we will look at some simple programming examples using ESL. You will need a phone connected to your FreeSWITCH server, and two terminal windows open so that you can look at your program in one session and `fs_cli` in another.

How to do it...

Consider a simple example. Here we will compare the event socket output before and after using a filter:

1. Launch `fs_cli` and connect to a running FreeSWITCH server. Issue these two commands at `fs_cli`:

    ```
    /log 0
    ```

    ```
    /event plain all
    ```

2. Wait a few seconds and no doubt you'll see some events, and possibly a lot of events.

3. From your phone, dial *98 and wait for the system to answer, then hang up. You should see many events.

4. Let's filter out everything except the channel hang up events. Issue this command:

    ```
    /filter Event-Name CHANNEL_HANGUP_COMPLETE
    ```

5. Repeat the call to *98, then hang up. You should see only a single event.

How it works...

FreeSWITCH uses a "filter in" system (as opposed to a "filter out" system) for filtering events. If no filters have been set then the event socket shows all events. The command we issued means, in effect, "Show all CHANNEL_HANGUP_COMPLETE events". You may set additional filters. For example:

```
/filter Event-Name CHANNEL_HANGUP_COMPLETE
/filter Event-Name CHANNEL_EXECUTE
```

These commands add two filters. In effect, they mean, "Show all CHANNEL_HANGUP_COMPLETE events and all CHANNEL_EXECUTE events". There is no limit to the number of filters you may set on an event socket connection.

The fs_cli is useful for looking at simple events and doing some basic debugging, but in practice you probably will need to apply filters from within a program.

Consider this functional Perl script:

```perl
use ESL;
my $con = new ESL::ESLconnection("localhost", "8021", "ClueCon");
if ( !$con ) {
    die "Unable to connect to FreeSWITCH server; $!\n";
}
$con->events('plain','all');
while (1) {
my $e = $con->recvEventTimed(10);
next unless $e;
print $e->serialize();
}
```

Though not particularly useful, this Perl script demonstrates how to connect to the FreeSWITCH event socket using ESL and listen for events. When it receives an event it will print it to the console. The $con variable is the ESL connection object and $e is an event object. Run this script on your system and you will see that it dumps every event. Let's add a filter and a few strategic print statements. Modify the script as follows:

```perl
$con->events('plain','all');
$con->filter('Event-Name','CHANNEL_STATE');
while (1) {
   my $e = $con->recvEventTimed(10);
   next unless $e;
   my $chan_state = $e->getHeader('Channel-State');
   my $chan_call_state = $e->getHeader('Channel-Call-State');
   my $chan_leg = $e->getHeader('Call-Direction') eq 'inbound' ? 'A' :
   'B';
```

```perl
    my $chan_name = $e->getHeader('Channel-Name');
    print "($chan_leg Leg) $chan_state / $chan_call_state
    [$chan_name]\n";
}
```

First, note that we add a filter on CHANNEL_STATE events. This will let us receive only events when there is a state change on a channel, for example, when a channel goes from "ringing" to "answered". We also create several Perl variables:

Variable	Purpose
$chan_state	Channel state (NEW, INIT, ROUTING)
$chan_call_state	Call state (RINGING, ACTIVE, HANGUP, DOWN)
$chan_leg	Call leg (A leg or B leg)
$chan_name	Channel name

Run this script on your system and then make a call from one phone to another. Watch the output while the target phone is ringing, then when the target phone is answered, and finally when one of the phones hangs up. Observing this process will help you grasp the types of events that FreeSWITCH throws as calls traverse the system.

See also

▸   The *Setting up the event socket library* recipe earlier in this chapter

Launching a call with an inbound event socket connection

Using an inbound event socket connection to launch a call is a common requirement for some applications, such as outbound IVRs. In a case like this it is advantageous to handle the generating of the calls in a non-blocking manner using the ESL connection object's `bgapi()` method. This recipe discusses how to use the `bgapi()` method with the corresponding "Background-Job UUID".

Getting ready

Be sure that you have configured ESL for your system and that you have followed the steps in *Establishing an inbound event socket connection* earlier in this chapter. The examples here are written in Perl but the principles apply to any ESL-enabled language. Of course, you will need a text editor and a SIP phone registered to your FreeSWITCH server in order to test this example.

How to do it...

Start by creating the new script:

1. Create the file `scripts/ib_bgapi.pl` in a text editor and add these lines:

```perl
#!/usr/bin/perl
use strict;
use warnings;
require ESL;

my $host = "localhost";
my $port = "8021";
my $pass = "ClueCon";
my $con  = new ESL::ESLconnection($host, $port, $pass);
if (! $con) { die "Unable to establish connection to
$host:$port\n"; }
$con->events("plain","all");

my $target = shift;
my $uuid = $con->api("create_uuid")->getBody();
my $res =
  $con->bgapi("originate","{origination_uuid=$uuid}$target 9664");
my $job_uuid = $res->getHeader("Job-UUID");
print "Call to $target has Job-UUID of $job_uuid and call uuid of
$uuid \n";

my $stay_connected = 1;
while ( $stay_connected ) {
  my $e = $con->recvEventTimed(0);
  if ( $e ) {
    my $ev_name = $e->getHeader("Event-Name");
    if ( $ev_name eq 'BACKGROUND_JOB' ) {
      my $call_result = $e->getBody();
      print "Result of call to $target was $call_result\n\n";
    } elsif ( $ev_name eq 'DTMF' ) {
      my $digit = $e->getHeader("DTMF-Digit");
      print "Received DTMF digit: $digit\n";
      if ( $digit =~ m/\D/ ) {
        print "Exiting...\n";
        $stay_connected = 0;
      }
    } else {
      # Some other event
    }
```

```
    } else {
      # do other things while waiting for events...
    }
  }
  $con->api("uuid_kill",$uuid);
```

2. Save the file and exit.

3. Linux/Unix users make the script executable with this command:

   chmod +x ib_bgapi.pl

4. Launch the script:

   Linux/Unix: `./ib_bgapi.pl` user/1000

   Windows: `perl.exe ib_bgapi.pl` user/1000

Be sure to replace "1000" with the extension number for your phone. Your phone should ring; when you answer you will hear music. Watch the console as you answer the call and press DTMF digits. Press * or # to exit the script.

How it works...

This script takes a dialstring as an argument on the command line and then makes a `bgapi` ("background API") origination attempt to that dialstring. Whenever `bgapi` is called there will always be a "Job-UUID" response. The `bgapi` command is discussed a little later. We use the `uuid_create` method of the ESL connection object to create a UUID that we can assign to our outbound call leg. Normally FreeSWITCH will assign a UUID value to each call leg, however by preselecting the UUID value we save ourselves some extra (unnecessary) parsing of events to try to decipher the UUID.

At this point we generate the outbound call, print some information about the call, and then enter our main event loop. Note these two lines:

```
  my $stay_connected = 1;
  while ( $stay_connected ) {
```

The `$stay_connected` variable is simply a flag, and as long as it evaluates to true then the event loop keeps running. The script then polls the event socket for events:

```
    my $e = $con->recvEventTimed(0);
```

The argument to `recvEventTimed` is the number of milliseconds to block while waiting for an event. By setting it to zero we are simply checking to see if there are events waiting in the event queue. The `$e` variable will evaluate to false if there were no events waiting:

```
if ( $e ) {
    ...
} else {
    # do other things while waiting for events...
}
```

The `else` block of this `if` statement can be used to let your code handle other operations while you are waiting for events to come. If an event does come in we have this `if` block to check the type of event:

```
my $ev_name = $e->getHeader("Event-Name");
if ( $ev_name eq 'BACKGROUND_JOB' ) {
    my $call_result = $e->getBody();
    print "Result of call to $target was $call_result\n\n";
} elsif ( $ev_name eq 'DTMF' ) {
    my $digit = $e->getHeader("DTMF-Digit");
    print "Received DTMF digit: $digit\n";
    if ( $digit =~ m/\D/ ) {
        print "Exiting...\n";
        $stay_connected = 0;
    }
} else {
    # Some other event
}
```

We examine the event name for BACKGROUND_JOB or DTMF in the `if` and `elsif` checks (highlighted). We also have a bare `else` block where we can handle events of other types if we choose to do so. When we receive our BACKGROUND_JOB event we display the result of the `originate` command. The rest of the script is spent in the event loop waiting for DTMF events. When a DTMF event comes in we display the key that the caller pressed. If the key is not a digit (* or #) then the script will exit, otherwise the event loop keeps on processing. Note: we explicitly hang up the channel using the `uuid_kill` command.

There's more...

You can learn more about the mechanics of using `bgapi` by issuing some simple commands at the `fs_cli`. Open an `fs_cli` session and try these commands:

```
/log 0
bgapi status
```

You will see a reply, something like this:

```
+OK Job-UUID: f719939a-ffa1-49ca-a8b6-7f080febc2dc
```

You can manually watch for BACKGROUND_JOB events with this fs_cli command:

```
/event plain background_job
```

Now issue another bgapi status command. In addition to the reply you will also see the actual BACKGROUND_JOB event. An abbreviated event looks like this:

```
Event-Name: [BACKGROUND_JOB]

...

Job-UUID: [f719939a-ffa1-49ca-a8b6-7f080febc2dc]
Job-Command: [status]
Content-Length: [177]
Content-Length: 177


UP 0 years, 0 days, 0 hours, 15 minutes, 2 seconds, 165 milliseconds, 501
microseconds
1 session(s) since startup
0 session(s) 0/90
1000 session(s) max
min idle cpu 0.00/100.00
```

The status command returns the BACKGROUND_JOB event immediately. However, the originate command will not return a BACKGROUND_JOB event until the originate API has succeeded (the call is answered) or fails (a busy, no answer, and so on). Try it with your phone:

```
bgapi originate user/1000 9664
```

Replace 1000 with the extension number of your phone. You will get the +OK reply back immediately, but you won't get the BACKGROUND_JOB event until the call is answered or goes to voicemail. One thing to keep in mind is that by default, if the far end sends back **early media** then the originate is considered successful, even if that early media is a busy signal, special information tone (SIT), or a ring with no-answer.

See also

▸ The *Setting up the event socket library, Establishing an inbound event socket connection,* and *Getting familiar with the fs_cli interface* recipes in this chapter

Using the ESL connection object for call control

Sometimes it is convenient (or even necessary) to control a call from a script. In such cases you can use the ESL connection object to control a call from an ESL script. This recipe will demonstrate a simple script that will answer a call, play a prompt, accept some caller input, and then route the call based upon that input. With these basic concepts demonstrated you will then be able to write custom scripts that meet your specific needs.

Getting ready

This recipe is an example of an "outbound" connection from the FreeSWITCH dialplan to an ESL script. As such, you should read *Establishing an outbound socket connection* earlier in this chapter. This recipe will require at least two terminal windows: one for `fs_cli` and one for the script. Although the script presented here is written in Perl, the connection object applies to all ESL-enabled languages.

How to do it...

First, add a new extension to your dialplan by following these steps:

1. Edit or create a new file in `conf/dialplan/default/` named `01_event_socket.xml`.

2. Add this extension to the new file:

   ```xml
   <extension name="ESL Con Obj Example">
     <condition field="destination_number" expression="^(996\d)$">
       <action application="log"
               data="INFO Starting ESL connection object example"/>
       <action application="socket"
               data="127.0.0.1:8040 sync full"/>
     </condition>
   </extension>
   ```

3. Save the file, exit, then issue `reloadxml` or press *F6* at the `fs_cli` prompt.

This extension will call your event socket script when the user dials **9960**. Create the following script or download it from the Packt Publishing website:

1. Create a new file in `scripts/` called `con_obj_example.pl`.

2. Add these lines:

   ```perl
   #!/usr/bin/perl
   use strict;
   ```

```perl
use warnings;
require ESL;
use IO::Socket::INET;
my $ip = "127.0.0.1";
my $sock = new IO::Socket::INET ( LocalHost => $ip,
                                  LocalPort => '8040',
                                  Proto => 'tcp',
                                  Listen => 1,
                                  Reuse => 1 );
die "Could not create socket: $!\n" unless $sock;
for(;;) {
  my $new_sock = $sock->accept();
  my $pid = fork();
  if ($pid > 0) {
    close($new_sock);
    next;
  } elsif ( $pid == 0 ) {
    my $host = $new_sock->sockhost();
    my $fd = fileno($new_sock);
    my $con = new ESL::ESLconnection($fd);
    my $info = $con->getInfo();
    my $uuid = $info->getHeader("unique-id");
    my $prompt = 'file_string://voicemail/vm-to_exit.wav';
    $prompt .= '!voicemail/vm-press.wav!digits/9.wav';
    $prompt .= ' ivr/ivr-that_was_an_invalid_entry.wav';
    $con->execute("answer");
    $con->execute("playback",
                  "ivr/ivr-welcome_to_freeswitch.wav");
    my $digits = "1";
    while($con->connected()) {
      while ( $digits != "9" && $con->connected() ) {
        $con->execute("play_and_get_digits",
                      "1 1 3 5000 # $prompt mydigits \\d+");
        my $e = $con->api("uuid_getvar","$uuid mydigits");
        $digits = $e->getBody();
        print "Received digit $digits\n";
        $con->execute("sleep","1000");
        $con->execute("playback","ivr/ivr-you_entered.wav");
        $con->execute("say","en number pronounced $digits");
        $con->execute("sleep","1000");
        if ( $digits == "9" ) {
          $con->execute("playback","voicemail/vm-goodbye.wav");
        }
      }
      $con->execute("hangup");
```

```
    }
    close($new_sock);
    exit(0);
  } else {
    die "Error forking new process: $!\n";
  }
}
```

3. Save the file and exit.

4. Make the script executable:

   chmod +x con_obj_example.pl

5. Run the script with this command:

   ./con_obj_example.pl

6. Once the script is running dial *9960* and follow the voice prompts.

How it works...

This script runs constantly—a daemon in Unix parlance—and waits for socket connections from FreeSWITCH on port 8040. As soon as a socket connection is established, the script **forks** a **child process**. This child process then creates the ESL connection object $con. Once the $con object is created we say a greeting to the caller and then enter the outer while loop. This loop causes the script to exit if the caller hangs up. The inner while loop uses the play_and_get_digits application to actually play the prompt and collect the digits from the caller. We then read back to the caller the digit he or she pressed using the say application. Finally, if the caller dialed the digit 9 then we say "goodbye", and then hang up. The child process then exits but the parent (the daemon) is still running. You can have multiple simultaneous calls in existence and each one will get its own process.

You can use this script as a template for creating your own interactive dialogs. All of the caller interactions take place within the inner while loop, so focus your attention there. Also, if you plan to play various sound prompts to the caller be sure to review the recipe *Use phrase macros to build sound prompts* in *Chapter 5*.

See also

> ▸ The *Setting up the event socket library, Establishing an outbound event socket connection,* and *Using fs_ivrd to manage outbound connections* recipes in this chapter

Using the built-in web interface

FreeSWITCH comes with a built-in web interface. It is made available by mod_xml_rpc, which is not loaded by default and therefore sometimes goes unnoticed.

Getting ready

You will need to make sure that mod_xml_rpc is built and loaded before trying to connect to the web interface. The mod_xml_rpc module is already compiled when using the Visual Studio 2008/2010 solution files with the FreeSWITCH source code. Linux and Mac OS X users will need to enable mod_xml_rpc in your FreeSWITCH installation. Follow these steps:

1. Open modules.conf in the FreeSWITCH source directory and remove the comment on the #xml_int/mod_xml_rpc line. Save the file and exit

2. Compile mod_xml_rpc with this command:

   make mod_xml_rpc-install

3. If you want to have mod_xml_rpc load automatically each time you start FreeSWITCH then edit conf/autoload_configs/modules.conf.xml and uncomment this line:

   ```
   <!-- <load module=" mod_xml_rpc "/> -->
   ```

   Save the file and exit.

4. If you do not load mod_xml_rpc automatically then simply load it with this command from fs_cli:

   load mod_xml_rpc

Once mod_xml_rpc is loaded you are ready to start using the web interface.

How to do it...

Follow these steps:

1. Connect to the web interface with a browser by opening a URL like http://x.x.x.x:8080, where x.x.x.x is the IP address of your FreeSWITCH server.

By default, the interface uses port 8080. When the server asks for a username and password enter "freeswitch" and "works" respectively. You will see a simple page displayed like this:

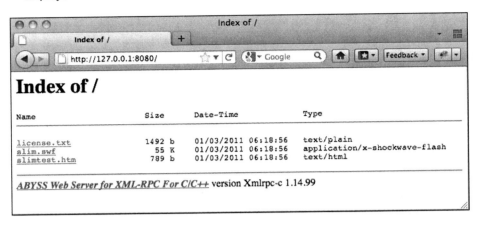

The files listed here are for the included Adobe Flash-based media player that lets you listen to audio sound files right from your browser and are not of particular note.

2. Let's send a simple command to FreeSWITCH. The syntax for sending a commands is: `http://x.x.x.x:8080/webapi/cmd?args`, where `x.x.x.x` is the IP address of FreeSWITCH, `cmd` is the API command to send, and `args` represents any arguments to the command. Assuming your IP address is 127.0.0.1, you can get the status of FreeSWITCH with the URL `http://127.0.0.1:8080/webapi/status`.

3. To view calls in progress use the URL `http://127.0.0.1:8080/webapi/show?channels`.

Any API command that you can type at `fs_cli` can also be sent via the web interface.

How it works...

FreeSWITCH features a clever design which anticipates the possibility that commands have been issued from the web-based interface instead of from the console or `fs_cli` utility. Commands that are "Web aware" will respond with HTML-formatted data. For example, the `help` command will respond with formatted output. Try sending this command from your browser: `http://127.0.0.1:8080/webapi/help`. Notice the table and alternating background colors. The `help` command is one of these "web-aware" commands. Note that not all commands are like this, so if you issue a command and the response does not seem formatted properly then try the `api` or `txtapi` alternatives. (The `api` method uses some formatting for the output whereas `txtapi` simply does a raw text dump for the output.) To get an idea of the differences, issue each of these commands and see the response: `http://127.0.0.1:8080/api/help` and `http://127.0.0.1:8080/txtapi/help`. You have a number of options for sending and receiving data using the built-in web server.

Be sure to change the default username and password before putting this feature into production. Look for the parameters `auth-user` and `auth-pass` in `conf/autoload_configs/xml_rpc.conf.xml`.

There's more...

The built-in web server is used for several interesting features.

Controlling PortAudio

If you have `mod_portaudio` installed then you will be happy to learn that there is a web interface for it. Browse to this URL `http://127.0.0.1:8080/webapi/pa` to see a simple form. While not particularly elegant, it demonstrates an alternative to using `fs_cli` to issue various `pa` commands. See *Using FreeSWITCH as a softphone* in *Chapter 2* for more information.

The "XML RPC" In mod_xml_rpc

This recipe has focused entirely on using a web browser to communicate with FreeSWITCH. However, it is entirely possible to use traditional XML RPC clients in various programming languages. If you are familiar with XML RPC programming then we recommend that you visit `http://wiki.freeswitch.org/wiki/Freeswitch_XML-RPC` to see some specific examples on using XML RPC. There is even an example for Drupal!

See also

▶   The *Listening to live calls with telecast* and *Using voicemail* recipes in *Chapter 5*

5
PBX Functionality

In this chapter, we will cover:

- ▶ Creating users
- ▶ Accessing voicemail
- ▶ Company directory
- ▶ Using phrase macros to build voice prompts
- ▶ Creating XML IVR menus
- ▶ Music on hold
- ▶ Creating conferences
- ▶ Sending faxes
- ▶ Receiving faxes
- ▶ Basic text-to-speech with `mod_flite`
- ▶ Advanced text-to-speech with `mod_tts_commandline`
- ▶ Listening to live calls with telecast
- ▶ Recording calls

Introduction

FreeSWITCH supports many features that are typically associated with a telephone system or **Private Branch Exchange** (**PBX**). The recipes in this chapter focus on a number of functions that are widely used in PBX systems such as voicemail, faxing, call recording, IVR menus, and more.

Historically, the term PBX refers to a specific type of telephone system. However, it is now commonly used as a general term for any type of telephone system.

Creating users

Each FreeSWITCH system has a directory of users. In most cases a user is the literal person who has a telephone. When we say that we are "adding a user" we mean that we are creating a user account in the directory of users. Each "user" has the SIP credentials for making outbound calls as well as a PIN number for accessing voicemail. In fact, you cannot have a voicemail box without having a corresponding user account.

Getting ready

At a minimum you will need a terminal window to issue commands to your system. To use the `add_user` script your system will need to have Perl installed.

How to do it...

There are two basic steps for creating a user. The steps are as follows:

1. Adding the user to the directory.
2. Adding the corresponding extension number to the dialplan.

Let's assume we have a fresh installation of FreeSWITCH, which means we have user ID's 1000 through 1019 (the `Local_Extension` in `conf/dialplan/default.xml` is set to route calls to those ID's).

Let's add a new user with these steps:

1. Open your terminal and `cd` into your FreeSWITCH source directory.
2. Linux users issue this command: `./scripts/perl/add_user 1020`.
3. Windows users do this: `perl scripts\perl\add_user 1020`.

You should see some output confirming the new user is created. Next we need to modify the `Local_Extension` in the `default` context. Perform these steps:

1. Open `conf/dialplan/default.xml` in a text editor.
2. Locate the dialplan extension named `Local_Extension`.
3. Change the expression from `^(10[01][0-9])$` to `^(10[012][0-9])$`.
4. Save the file and exit. Then issue a `reloadxml` command from the `fs_cli`.

User 1020 is now ready for use. To test, have a SIP phone register as user "1020" and then call it from another phone.

How it works...

The `add_user` script simply adds a new file in the directory. In the case of user ID 1020, it literally created the file `conf/directory/default/1020.xml`. Once that file is created (and you've issued a `reloadxml` command) then a SIP phone can register as that user. However, the dialplan isn't by default set up to handle someone dialing *1020*, which is why we had to update the `Local_Extension` in `default.xml`. The default `<condition>` for the `Local_Extension` is:

```
<condition field="destination_number" expression="^(10[01][0-9])$">
```

This pattern matches 1000, 1001, ... 1019. We changed the `<condition>` line to read as follows:

```
<condition field="destination_number" expression="^(10[012][0-9])$">
```

Our new pattern adds 1020, 1021, ... 1029 to the `Local_Extension`. Why the whole range instead of just "1020"? There is nothing preventing you from doing that, however it is quite common to add users in blocks and not one at a time. If you prefer, you could use the following pattern:

```
<condition field="destination_number" expression="^(10[01][0-
9]|1020)$">
```

As mentioned, though, this means that if you want to add user 1021 then you would need to come back and change this regular expression pattern again.

There's more...

The `add_users` script has many useful features (run `add_users --help` to see the full set of options). One such feature is adding a block of users. For example, if we wanted to complete the block of 1020, 1021, ... 1029 we need not run the script for each user to add. Instead, specify a range with the `--users` argument:

```
./scripts/perl/add_user --users=1020-1029
```

Note that the `add_user` script will not overwrite existing users.

Regular expressions with Regexp::Assemble

You may have seen a message like this on the screen after running the `add_user` script:

```
If CPAN module Regexp::Assemble were installed this program would be able
to suggest a regex for your new users.
```

If you install the CPAN module `Regexp::Assemble` then the `add_user` script will suggest a regular expression pattern. A quick way to install this module from the command line is by using the following command:

```
perl -MCPAN -e 'install Regexp::Assemble'
```

Now when you add a user the script will suggest a regular expression pattern. Note that this is merely a suggestion—you should still verify your pattern to make sure it addresses your needs.

See also

▶ Refer to the *Configuring a SIP phone to register with FreeSWITCH* recipe in *Chapter 2*

Accessing voicemail

Voicemail is a very common feature for PBX systems. This recipe shows how to access voicemail for a user.

Getting ready

You will need at least one telephone registered on your system, although it is easier to test with two or more phones. Have another user call. The destination extension should let the call go to voicemail. The caller should leave a message and hang up. Once a message is left, the target phone can access voicemail.

How to do it...

The simplest way to access voicemail is to simply dial *98 on the phone. The system will ask for the user ID and then the password (by default the password is the same as the user ID). Let's assume that user 1001 is checking her voicemail messages. She would follow these steps:

1. Dial *98, wait for system to answer.
2. Enter the ID and press # (1001# in our example).
3. Enter the password and press # (1001# in our example).
4. New messages are automatically played.

Simply hang up the phone to exit from voicemail.

How it works...

The voicemail system really is nothing more than a specific type of IVR system. In this case the user can log in and has several choices. The main menu options are as follows:

Key	Action
1	Listen to new messages
2	Listen to saved messages
5	Advanced options
#	Exit voicemail

While listening to new or saved messages the user has these options:

Key	Action
1	Listen to the message from the beginning
2	Save message
4	Rewind
6	Fast forward
7	Delete
0	Pause playback
*	Skip the envelope information (Date/time and sender)

After the message has been played the options are:

Key	Action
1	Listen to the message from the beginning
2	Save message
7	Delete

The advanced menu options are:

Key	Action
1	Record greeting
2	Choose greeting
3	Record name
6	Change password
0	Main menu

Most users will find the FreeSWITCH voicemail system very familiar as it is modelled on the voicemail systems used by most major mobile phone carriers.

See also

▸ Refer to the *Configuring a SIP phone to register with FreeSWITCH* recipe in *Chapter 2*

Company directory

Most companies have some form of dial-by-name directory. This recipe will show you how to add a company directory to your FreeSWITCH installation using `mod_directory`.

How to do it...

Enable and build `mod_directory` by following these steps:

1. Open `freeswitch_src/modules.conf` in a text editor.
2. Uncomment this line:

   `#applications/mod_directory`

3. Save the file and exit.
4. Linux/Unix users issue the proper `make` command:

   make mod_directory-install

Allow `mod_directory` to be loaded when FreeSWITCH starts:

1. Open `conf/autoload_configs/modules.conf.xml` in a text editor.
2. Uncomment this line:

   `<!--<load module="mod_directory"/>-->`

3. Save the file and exit.
4. Restart FreeSWITCH.
5. Start `fs_cli` and issue the command `show application`.

You should see an application named **directory** in the list. Next we need to add a simple dialplan extension that will let us test:

1. Open `conf/dialplan/default/01_Custom.xml` in a text editor.

2. Add these lines:

```
<extension name="dial by name">
  <condition field="destination_number" expression="^(1411)$">
    <action application="directory" data="default ${domain}"/>
  </condition>
</extension>
```

3. Save the file and exit.

The last thing to do is to make sure that at least one user in the directory has the `directory_full_name` or `effective_caller_id_name` variable set in the directory entry. For now we will set the `directory_full_name` on user 1000:

1. Open `conf/directory/default/1000.xml` in a text editor.

2. Add this line to the `<variables>` section:

```
<variable name="directory_full_name" value="Ada Lovelace"/>
```

3. Save the file and exit. Press *F6* or issue the `reloadxml` command from `fs_cli`.

At this point you are ready to test. Dial *1411* from your phone and listen to the options. For this test, dial the first three letters of the last name (*568* for "L-O-V") and listen to the results.

How it works...

The `directory` application gets its information from the user directory. By using the `directory_full_name` variable we specify the first and last names for purposes of searching the user directory. You can also use the `effective_caller_id_name` variable if you wish. The latter variable controls the caller ID name displayed when the user makes outbound calls. If for any reason this is not the name you want searched then use `directory_full_name`, which will always supersede `effective_caller_id_name` for dial-by-name searches.

Most likely in your initial test you did not hear someone's voice saying, "Ada Lovelace" but rather you heard the system spelling out the name. This is how `mod_directory` handles the case where the user has not recorded his or her name. If you log in to the voicemail system and record a name prompt (option 5 from the VM main menu, then option 3) then the system will use that recording instead of spelling out the user's name.

There's more...

You have two parameters that you can set for each user to customize the behavior of the directory application:

▸ `directory-visible`: Set this parameter to `false` to prevent the user from being included in directory searches. This is useful for keeping the directory from being cluttered with entries like "hallway phone", and "guest phone". It is also handy for keeping VIP extensions from being included.

▸ `directory-exten-visible`: Set this parameter to `false` to prevent the `directory` application from voicing the target user's extension number (some operations prefer to keep extension numbers from being public).

Both of the above parameters default to `true`, so keep that in mind as you are building your user database.

See also

▸ Refer to the *Accessing voicemail* and *Creating users* recipes in this chapter

Using phrase macros to build sound prompts

It is frequently necessary to piece together smaller sound recordings to create longer ones. The FreeSWITCH phrase macro system is a very powerful tool for not only piecing together individual sound files, but also for adding a little bit of logic so that your phrases are more than the mere amalgamation of individual sound prompts.

Getting ready

You will need a text editor and at least one SIP phone for this recipe. It is also recommended that you review the phrase file for your language. For English this is found in the FreeSWITCH source directory in `docs/phrase/phrase_en.xml`. The `phrase_en.xml` file contains both the file name of each pre-recorded prompt as well as the actual spoken text. Prompts are divided into sections such as `voicemail`, `IVR`, `currency`, `digits`, and `time`. By far the largest collection of sound prompts is in the `IVR` section.

In this recipe we will create a simple dialplan extension that will read back to the caller his extension number. We will use a phrase macro to handle the work of stitching together sound prompts and utilizing the `say` application to read back the caller's extension number.

How to do it...

Start by adding the extension to the dialplan:

1. Create or edit the file `conf/dialplan/default/01_Custom.xml`.

2. Add these lines:

```
<extension name="who's calling">
  <condition field="destination_number" expression="^(1500)$">
    <action application="answer"/>
    <action application="playback"
           data="phrase:whoami:${username}"/>
    <action application="hangup"/>
  </condition>
</extension>
```

3. Save the file and exit.

Next, create the phrase macro:

1. Create or edit the file `conf/lang/en/ivr/custom.xml`.

2. Add these lines:

```
<macro name="whoami">
  <input pattern="^(\d+)$">
    <match>
      <action function="play-file"
             data="ivr/ivr-extension_number.wav"/>
      <action function="sleep"
             data="100"/>
      <action function="say"
             data="$1"
             method="pronounced"
             type="number"/>
    </match>
    <nomatch>
      <action function="play-file"
             data="ivr/ivr-that_was_an_invalid_entry.wav"/>
    </nomatch>
  </input>
</macro>
```

3. Save the file and exit.

4. Issue the `reloadxml` command (or press *F6*) at the `fs_cli`.

Test the new extension by dialing *1500*.

How it works...

The key to this operation is this line in the dialplan extension we created:

```
<action application="playback"
    data="phrase:whoami:${username}"/>
```

The playback application normally takes a file name as an argument. However, if the argument begins with `phrase:` then playback will look for a phrase macro instead of an audio file. In this case, we call a phrase macro named `whoami` and give it the argument of `${username}`, which contains the ID number of the calling user. At this point the phrase macro takes control.

The argument passed to the macro gets handled with this line:

```
<input pattern="^(\d+)$">
```

The input value is matched against the regular expression in the `pattern` option. In most cases `${username}` contains only digits, so our pattern will capture those into the special variable `$1`. At this point we now have a bit of logic to help decide what to do. If the input matches the pattern, then the actions inside of the `<match>` node will be executed. If there is not a match then the actions inside of the `<nomatch>` node will be executed (in the rare case of a non-user calling extension 1500 we simply play a message that says, **That was an invalid entry**).

You have probably figured out by now that the actions contained inside of the `match` (or `nomatch`) are executed sequentially. You can also see that phrase macros are not merely limited to playing individual sound files. You can call functions like `sleep` and `say` to customize the way the prompt is played to the user. You can even call a `text-to-speech` application if you have one installed.

There's more...

It is possible to execute many different operations using phrase macros. In fact, the FreeSWITCH voicemail system uses phrase macros extensively. Look through `conf/lang/en/vm/sounds.xml` to see all the different phrase macros that `mod_voicemail` uses. Keep in mind that you can use any of the phrase macros in `sounds.xml` as long as you call them with the correct arguments.

One particularly useful phrase macro is called `voicemail_record_file_check`. Consider the case where you are asking the caller to record a prompt. Perhaps you have a custom application and the caller needs to record a prompt. This macro allows you to have a custom phrase that says something like "press 1 to listen, press 2 to save, press 3 to re-record." As an example, you could use `play_and_get_digits` to tell the caller what to do:

```
<action application="play_and_get_digits" data="1 1 3 4000 #
phrase:voicemail_record_file_check:1:2:3 ivr/ivr-invalid_entry.wav
selection \d"/>
```

The above action would literally tell the caller, "Press 1 to listen to the recording; press 2 to save the recording; press 3 to re-record". It would then capture the input into channel variable ${selection}. Note that the options voiced to the caller are customizable with this macro. Calling the macro with phrase:voicemail_record_file_check:4:5:6 would literally tell the caller, "Press 4 to listen to the recording; press 5 to save the recording; press 6 to re-record".

A good way to learn more about phrase macros is to watch the console while calling in to voicemail as you will be able to watch in real-time as FreeSWITCH parses the phrase macro and performs the actions therein.

See also

> ▶ Refer to the *Basic text-to-speech with mod_flite* and *Advanced text-to-speech with mod_tts_commandline* recipes later in this chapter

Creating XML IVR menus

FreeSWITCH has a simple but flexible system for building IVR-style menus for caller interaction. In this recipe we create a custom menu that is very similar to the demo IVR that is part of the default FreeSWITCH configuration.

Getting ready

You will need a text editor and a telephone for testing. We will create a custom menu for extension number 5002 and we will use a generic greeting that comes with the FreeSWITCH sound files. To use the dial-by-name directory be sure to complete the recipe *Company directory* earlier in this chapter.

How to do it...

Create the menu definition by following these steps:

1. Open a text editor and create a new file called conf/ivr_menus/custom_ivr.xml.
2. Add these lines:

```
<menu name="simple_greeting"
       greet-long="ivr/ivr-generic_greeting.wav"
       greet-short="ivr/ivr-generic_greeting.wav"
       invalid-sound="ivr/ivr-that_was_an_invalid_entry.wav"
       exit-sound="voicemail/vm-goodbye.wav"
       confirm-attempts="3"
       timeout="10000"
       inter-digit-timeout="2000"
```

```
                max-failures="3"
                max-timeouts="3"
                digit-len="4">
        <entry action="menu-exec-app" digits="9"
                param="directory default ${domain}"/>
        <entry action="menu-exec-app"
                digits="/^(10[01][0-9])$/"
                param="transfer $1 XML features"/>
        <entry action="menu-top" digits="*"/>
    </menu>
```

3. Save the file.

Next, create a simple extension that lets us test our menu:

1. Open `conf/dialplan/default/01_Custom.xml` in a text editor.

2. Add this extension:

```
<extension name="sample greeting">
  <!-- Good morning 12am to 11:59 -->
  <condition hour="0-11" break="never">
    <action application="set" data="tod=morning" inline="true"/>
  </condition>
  <!-- Good afternoon 12pm to 17:59 -->
  <condition hour="12-17" break="never">
    <action application="set" data="tod=afternoon" inline="true"/>
  </condition>
  <!-- Good morning 18:00 to 23:59 -->
  <condition hour="18-23" break="never">
    <action application="set" data="tod=evening" inline="true"/>
  </condition>
  <condition field="destination_number" expression="^5002$">
    <action application="answer"/>
    <action application="sleep" data="1000"/>
    <action application="playback"
            data="ivr/ivrgood_${tod}.wav"/>
    <action application="sleep" data="500"/>
    <action application="ivr" data="simple_greeting"/>
  </condition>
</extension>
```

3. Save the file and exit.

4. Issue the `reloadxml` command (or press *F6*) at the `fs_cli`.

Test your new extension by dialing *5002*.

How it works...

While this is a minimal example of creating a menu, it is still a very useful example of how to create a simple "main greeting" for a company's PBX.

There's more...

Many times it is beneficial to use a phrase macro with an IVR menu. For example, in our dialplan we manually compute the time of day and voice it to the caller. We then launch the `ivr` application with our generic greeting. This is not optimal for a few reasons. First off, having a simple `.wav` file for our greeting means that we are stuck with whatever is recorded. Secondly, using a phrase macro gives us a bit more flexibility in how we use our macros. Let's improve our menu by using a phrase macro. Our goals will be as follows:

- ▸ Add "To repeat these options, press *" to our greeting
- ▸ Skip the "Good morning/afternoon/evening" when repeating our options
- ▸ Clean up the readability of our dialplan

As you will see, using a phrase macro accomplishes all of this and more. First, let's clean up the dialplan. Open `conf/dialplan/default/01_Custom.xml` and edit our extension so that it has only these lines:

```
<extension name="sample greeting">
  <condition field="destination_number" expression="^5002$">
    <action application="answer"/>
    <action application="ivr" data="simple_greeting"/>
  </condition>
</extension>
```

Now let's create a separate extension that always gets executed at the beginning of the dialplan. Normally you do this at the beginning of the `default` context. Open `conf/dialplan/default.xml` and add this as the first extension in the default context:

```
<extension name="set_tod" continue="true">
  <!-- Good morning 12am to 11:59 -->
  <condition hour="0-11" break="never">
    <action application="set"
            data="tod=morning"
            inline="true"/>
  </condition>
  <!-- Good afternoon 12pm to 17:59 -->
  <condition hour="12-17" break="never">
    <action application="set"
            data="tod=afternoon"
            inline="true"/>
```

```
        </condition>
      <!-- Good morning 18:00 to 23:59 -->
      <condition hour="18-23" break="never">
        <action application="set"
                data="tod=evening"
                inline="true"/>
      </condition>
    </extension>
```

Adding this extension to the dialplan allows all calls in the `default` context to have the `tod` channel variable set. This in turn lets any extension (or script, or phrase macro) have access to `tod`, not just our custom extension.

Next, open `conf/ivr_menus/custom_ivr.xml` and change these two lines to use our macro:

```
        greet-long="phrase:simple_greeting:long"
        greet-short="phrase:simple_greeting:short"
```

Finally, add the new macro. It's a bit long, however it accomplishes a lot for us. Open `conf/lang/en/ivr/custom.xml` and add a new macro:

```
    <macro name="simple_greeting">
      <input pattern="^(long)$" break-on-match="true">
        <match>
          <action function="sleep"
                  data="1000"/>
          <action function="play-file"
                  data="ivr/ivr-good_${tod}.wav"/>
          <action function="sleep"
                  data="500"/>
          <action function="play-file"
                  data="ivr/ivr-generic_greeting.wav"/>
          <action function="sleep"
                  data="500"/>
          <action function="play-file"
                  data="ivr/ivr-to_repeat_these_options.wav"/>
          <action function="sleep"
                  data="250"/>
          <action function="play-file"
                  data="voicemail/vm-press.wav"/>
          <action function="sleep"
                  data="100"/>
          <action function="play-file"
                  data="ascii/42.wav"/>
        </match>
```

```
    </input>
    <input pattern="^(short)$">
      <match>
        <action function="play-file"
                data="ivr/ivr-generic_greeting.wav"/>
        <action function="sleep"
                data="500"/>
        <action function="play-file"
                data="ivr/ivr-to_repeat_these_options.wav"/>
        <action function="sleep"
                data="250"/>
        <action function="play-file"
                data="voicemail/vm-press.wav"/>
        <action function="sleep"
                data="100"/>
        <action function="play-file"
                data="ascii/42.wav"/>
      </match>
    </input>
  </macro>
```

After saving all of the files press *F6* or issue the `reloadxml` command from `fs_cli`. Try calling 5002 and this time press * to repeat the options. On a repeat, the system will not say, "Good morning", and so on. In addition to being more functional, the phrase macro method also makes it easier for you to make changes to the greeting that you play to your callers.

See also

▶ Refer to the *Company directory* recipe earlier in this chapter

Music on hold

Music on hold (MOH) is a common feature of modern phone systems. FreeSWITCH allows you to have many different MOH selections.

Getting ready

You will need some music files if you wish to customize the MOH. Also, if you have MP3 files that you would like to use for MOH then you will need a utility that can convert them into standard WAV files. A freely available tool can be found at `http://www.mpg123.de`. You will also need a text editor and a telephone connected to your FreeSWITCH server.

How to do it...

The first thing to do is to install the default MOH files from the FreeSWITCH download site. The Linux/Unix users can issue the following command from the FreeSWITCH source directory:

```
make cd-moh-install
```

On Windows, the sound files are installed automatically as part of the MSVC solution file.

Once the sounds are installed you can confirm that they work by dialing *9664* (no `reloadxml` or system restart is necessary).

How it works...

The `make` command issued above installs the MOH files in 8 kHz, 16 kHz, 32 kHz, and 48 kHz sampling rates (the Windows build automatically installs these as well). The default dialplan extension number 9664 (9MOH) will play the default music on hold files to the caller. The music is supplied by the module `mod_file_stream`. It is possible to customize the MOH on your system by adding other streams.

There's more...

Let's create an alternative MOH source and test it out. If you have a few MP3 or WAV files that you would like to use then be ready to copy them over to a new subdirectory on the FreeSWITCH server. In this example, we will download a few pieces of royalty-free music along with an attribution sound clip and then we will convert them to WAV files using the `mpg123` tool.

Start by creating a directory for our new sounds. In Linux/Unix do this:

```
mkdir /usr/local/freeswitch/sounds/music/custom1
cd /usr/local/freeswitch/sounds/music/custom1
```

Copy your MP3 files into this directory. Alternatively you can download some royalty free music at:

```
wget http://music.incompetech.com/royalty-free/Skye%20Cuillin.mp3
wget http://music.incompetech.com/royalty-free/Parisian.mp3
wget http://music.incompetech.com/royalty-free/credits%20sounder.mp3
```

Now convert your MP3 files to WAV files and remove the MP3 files.

```
for i in *.mp3; do mpg123 -m -r 8000 -w "`basename "$i" .mp3`".wav "$i";
done
rm *.mp3
```

You now have a set of 8 kHz WAV files that can be used as a music source. The next step is to create the actual file stream.

Open `conf/autoload_configs/local_stream.conf.xml` and add this new stream definition:

```
<directory name="custom1" path="$${sounds_dir}/music/custom1">
   <param name="rate" value="8000"/>
   <param name="shuffle" value="true"/>
   <param name="channels" value="1"/>
   <param name="interval" value="20"/>
   <param name="timer-name" value="soft"/>
</directory>
```

Save the file and close. Open `conf/dialplan/default/01_Custom.xml` and add this extension:

```
<extension name="hold_music">
   <condition field="destination_number" expression="^96642$">
     <action application="playback" data="${custom1}"/>
   </condition>
</extension>
```

Save the file and close. Lastly we need to create the `${custom1}` global variable that can be used anywhere we want to play our custom MOH. Open `conf/vars.xml` in a text editor and add this line:

```
<X-PRE-PROCESS cmd="set" data="custom1=local_stream://custom1"/>
```

Save the file and exit. Go to `fs_cli` and issue `reloadxml` or press *F6*.

When changing local stream definitions you need to reload the `local_stream` module from `fs_cli`:

reload mod_local_stream

When the module is reloaded, issue this command:

show_local_stream

Among the local streams listed should be your new "custom1" stream:

```
custom1,/usr/local/freeswitch/sounds/music/custom1
```

Now you may dial *96642* and you should hear your new music source.

You may now use `${custom1}` as the source of MOH, sound supplied in for ringback, and transfer ringback operations.

Creating conferences

FreeSWITCH excels at letting multiple parties connect to a single conference "room" where they can all hear and speak to one another. The default configuration has some examples of conferences that we can use as a starting point. Keep in mind that in FreeSWITCH there is no need explicitly to "create" a conference room—the `conference` dialplan application does all the work for us.

Getting ready

In addition to having a text editor you will need at least two phones for testing, and preferably another person or two so that you can verify that your conference rooms are working. Also, make sure that you have the default FreeSWITCH configuration installed as well as the sound and music files.

How to do it...

Follow these steps:

1. Dial *3000* and listen. You will be put into a standard conference room, and if you are the only person there you will hear hold music.

2. Dial *3000* from another phone and both persons are in the conference.

3. Add more parties by dialing *3000*.

How it works...

The default FreeSWITCH dialplan has conferences pre-defined and ready for use (note that the conferences are not actually "active" until at least one person calls in). The default dialplan has these conference extensions:

Extension Range	Conference Audio Sampling Rate
3000-3099	8 kHz
3100-3199	16 kHz
3200-3299	32 kHz
3300-3399	48 kHz

The sampling rate is the maximum sampling rate for all members. For example if you have a phone that uses G.722 at 16 kHz and you call into 3000 then your audio will be resampled to 8 kHz before being sent out to the other participants. If you have multiple parties whose phones support wide-band audio, then be sure to use a conference room with a higher sampling rate to take advantage of the higher quality audio.

If you simply need to have several people all hear each other in a conference room, then use the conference extensions in the default dialplan and modify the extension numbers as needed.

There's more...

Conferences support many features, such as caller controls and moderators. Read on for information about using these other features.

Caller controls

There are many controls that you can give to callers in a conference. The most common ones are as follows:

- ▸ **Talk volume**: The volume of the audio the caller sends (that is, gain control).
- ▸ **Listen volume**: The volume of the audio the caller hears.
- ▸ **Energy threshold**: The minimum energy level of the audio from the caller to be considered talking. Raising the energy level will cut down on background noise when a participant is in a noisy environment.

To see the default controls, open `conf/autoload_configs/conference.conf.xml` and locate the following section:

```
<caller-controls>
  <group name="default">
    <control action="mute" digits="0"/>
    <control action="deaf mute" digits="*"/>
    <control action="energy up" digits="9"/>
    <control action="energy equ" digits="8"/>
    <control action="energy dn" digits="7"/>
    <control action="vol talk up" digits="3"/>
    <control action="vol talk zero" digits="2"/>
    <control action="vol talk dn" digits="1"/>
    <control action="vol listen up" digits="6"/>
    <control action="vol listen zero" digits="5"/>
    <control action="vol listen dn" digits="4"/>
    <control action="hangup" digits="#"/>
  </group>
</caller-controls>
```

The name of this call control group is "default" and it cannot be modified. However, you can define your own custom caller controls and then add them to your conference definitions. Each conference is defined by a "profile" in the `<profiles>` section of `conference.conf.xml`. Let's say you created a caller control group named "custom". To set the conference profile to use those controls just add this parameter to the profile:

```
<param name="caller-controls" value="custom"/>
```

Now all callers who join this conference will have your custom caller controls.

Conference moderator and PIN

Some conferences have the concept of a "moderator" who has some level of control over the conference. In FreeSWITCH, the conference moderator is simply a conference member whose absence or presence can optionally affect the conference. There are two primary ways the moderator affects the conference:

▸ All members wait until the moderator arrives

▸ The conference ends (all members disconnected) when the moderator leaves

A moderator is created by modifying the conference application's argument in the dialplan. Compare these two lines:

```
<action application="conference" data="$1@default"/>
<action application="conference" data="$1@default+flags{moderator}"/>
```

Notice that we add "+flags{moderator}" to set the caller as the moderator. You can have multiple flags separated by commas, for example, "+flags{moderator,mute}".

Adding a PIN to the conference is simple as well. The same two conferences listed above can have a PIN added like this:

```
<action application="conference" data="$1@default+1234"/>
<action application="conference"
        data="$1@default+1234+flags{moderator}"/>
```

In both cases, the conference PIN is "1234" and the caller will not be allowed into the conference until he or she enters the correct PIN number.

Sending faxes

FreeSWITCH can transmit electronic documents to a destination fax machine. Only TIFF documents can be transmitted, however it is possible to convert a number of graphical formats to TIFF. This recipe will discuss some common and freely available tools.

Getting ready

In simple terms, sending a fax requires only a few things such as a TIFF file, a gateway, and a destination fax machine (for testing purposes you can download the sample TIFF file at `http://files.freeswitch.org/txfax-sample.tiff`). Put your TIFF file in a known location. For our example we will use `/tmp/txfax-sample.tiff`. The gateway is your connection to the outside world and the fax machine will simply be the device that answers your outbound phone call. If you do not have a gateway or a fax machine handy you can still try out this recipe by using the `fax_receive` extension in the default dialplan.

How to do it...

In most cases involving fax transmissions you will make an outbound call to a fax machine (A leg) and then execute the `txfax` dialplan application. Execute these steps to send a simple fax transmission:

1. Launch `fs_cli`.
2. Execute this command:

   ```
   originate loopback/9178 &txfax(/tmp/txfax-sample.tiff)
   ```

Watch the console and eventually the fax transmission should successfully finish.

How it works...

The `originate` command creates the outbound leg of the fax call. In this example, we are literally making a call within our own FreeSWITCH server by using the `loopback` channel. The target extension is "9178". In a real example we would, of course, be dialing an external number. For example, we could do this:

```
originate sofia/gateway/my_gw/18005551212 &txfax(/tmp/txfax-sample.tiff)
```

In any case, once the A leg is answered, the `txfax` application is called. If all goes well, the fax transmission should go through and a received file will be found in `/tmp/rxfax.tiff`.

There's more...

Faxing can be tricky. The following sections offer some helpful suggestions.

Detecting a fax machine and responding

In some cases you may be making automated phone calls and you would like to react to a fax machine. Perhaps you would like to send a fax if a fax machine is detected, but would otherwise like to process the call normally. This can be accomplished with the `execute_on_fax_detect` channel variable. Consider this dialplan snippet:

```
<extension name="fax detect test">
  <condition field="destination_number" expression="1234">
    <action application="export"
            data="execute_on_fax_detect='execute_extension 9178'"/>
    <action application="bridge" data="loopback/9664"/>
  </condition>
</extension>
```

Here we tell the system to execute an extension (9178) if we detect a fax tone, otherwise the bridge happens normally and plays hold music. You can adapt this principle for use in your own dialplans. Simply create a "fax handler" extension and use `execute_extension` with `execute_on_fax_detect` to execute the handler extension whenever a fax machine is detected.

Diagnosing fax issues

The fax problems are quite common, especially in a VoIP environment. When a fax transmission fails for some reason it helps to know what happened. If you are using XML CDRs you will automatically have a number of channel variables populated on every fax call, whether successful or not. Here is a sample:

```
<fax_v17_disabled>0</fax_v17_disabled>
<fax_ecm_requested>1</fax_ecm_requested>
<fax_filename>/tmp/txfax.tif</fax_filename>
<fax_success>1</fax_success>
<fax_result_code>0</fax_result_code>
<fax_result_text>OK</fax_result_text>
<fax_ecm_used>on</fax_ecm_used>
<fax_local_station_id>SpanDSP%20Fax%20Ident</fax_local_station_id>
<fax_remote_station_id>SpanDSP%20Fax%20Ident</fax_remote_station_id>
<fax_document_transferred_pages>1</fax_document_transferred_pages>
<fax_document_total_pages>1</fax_document_total_pages>
<fax_image_resolution>8031x3850</fax_image_resolution>
<fax_image_size>24111</fax_image_size>
<fax_bad_rows>0</fax_bad_rows>
<fax_transfer_rate>14400</fax_transfer_rate>
```

Use this information to diagnose your fax issues.

Helpful software

There are numerous **Free and Open Source Software** (**FOSS**) packages that are available to help with handling PDF and TIFF files. Members of the FreeSWITCH community have had particular success with Ghost Script (http://pages.cs.wisc.edu/~ghost/), which lets you convert to and from PDF and PostScript files.

A common operation is to convert a PDF file to TIFF before transmitting via fax. The following command will make a standard resolution TIFF file from the source PDF:

```
gs -q -r204x98 -g1728x1078 -dNOPAUSE -dBATCH -dSAFER -sDEVICE=tiffg3
-sOutputFile=txfax.tiff -- txfax.pdf
```

For a higher resolution file, use this command:

```
gs -q -r204x196 -g1728x2156 -dNOPAUSE -dBATCH -dSAFER -sDEVICE=tiffg3
-sOutputFile=txfax.tiff -- txfax.pdf
```

The Ghost Script executable (gs) is suited quite well to shell scripting.

See also

- ▶ Refer to the *Receiving faxes* recipe in this chapter
- ▶ Refer to the *Using XML CDRs* recipe in *Chapter 3*

Receiving faxes

The preceding recipe described the process of sending a fax. This recipe will describe the process of receiving a fax.

Getting ready

In its simplest format, receiving a fax requires only that you route an incoming call to an extension that then executes the rxfax dialplan application. As with the previous recipe, we can use our FreeSWITCH server to be both the sender and receiver of the fax. For our test we will use the same file we used in the *Sending faxes* recipe: /tmp/txfax-sample.tiff.

How to do it...

Execute these steps to do a simple fax transmission and reception:

1. Launch fs_cli.
2. Execute this command:

    ```
    originate loopback/9178 &txfax(/tmp/txfax-sample.tiff)
    ```

Watch the console and eventually the fax transmission should successfully finish.

How it works...

We use the `fax_receive` extension in the default dialplan to receive the fax transmission. This extension is quite simple:

```
<extension name="fax_receive">
  <condition field="destination_number" expression="^9178$">
    <action application="answer" />
    <action application="playback" data="silence_stream://2000"/>
    <action application="rxfax" data="/tmp/rxfax.tif"/>
    <action application="hangup"/>
  </condition>
</extension>
```

The received fax is stored in `/tmp/rxfax.tif`. Feel free to modify the filename. For example, if you have a `faxes/` subdirectory off the main `freeswitch` install directory you could do this:

```
<action application="rxfax" data="${base_dir}/faxes/${uuid}.tif"/>
```

Each incoming fax would have a unique file name and be stored in the `faxes/` subdirectory.

There's more...

Receiving faxes is usually part of a larger process or system. The following sections have some useful information for handling inbound fax transmissions.

Detecting inbound faxes

Let's say that you have an automated attendant that answers all incoming calls and lets callers choose their destinations. Occasionally a fax call may come in. Instead of disconnecting, you can detect the fax and send the call to a fax handler extension for processing. Add this extension to the part of your dialplan that processes inbound phone calls:

```
<extension name="fax detect" continue="true">
  <condition>
    <action application="set"
            data="execute_on_fax_detect=execute_extension handle_
incoming_fax"/>
  </condition>
</extension>
```

Now add an extension that actually handles the incoming faxes:

```
<extension name="fax_receive">
  <condition field="destination_number"
            expression="^handle_incoming_fax$">
```

```
      <action application="playback" data="silence_stream://2000"/>
      <action application="rxfax"
              data="${base_dir}/faxes/${uuid}.tif"/>
      <action application="hangup"/>
    </condition>
  </extension>
```

Now the system will automatically handle incoming faxes.

Processing a received fax

Once a fax is received it rarely needs just to sit in a directory somewhere. Usually you will want a person to see that fax transmission. A common practice is to convert the TIFF file into a PDF and then email the PDF as an attachment. Also, users appreciate it when caller ID information can be placed in the subject line of the e-mail. Keep in mind that this will only work if you have a properly configured **mail transport agent** (**MTA**) on your system. Modify your fax receive extension to be like this:

```
  <extension name="fax_receive">
    <condition field="destination_number"
               expression="^handle_incoming_fax$">
      <action application="set"
              data="api_hangup_hook=system
                    ${base_dir}/scripts/emailfax.sh
                    ${fax_remote_station_id}
                    ${base_dir}/faxes/${uuid}.tif"/>
      <action application="playback" data="silence_stream://2000"/>
      <action application="rxfax"
              data="${base_dir}/faxes/${uuid}.tif"/>
      <action application="hangup"/>
    </condition>
  </extension>
```

Note that we've added an api_hangup_hook to the fax receive extension. This will cause the script emailfax.sh to be executed. Create this script in a text editor and add these lines:

```
#!/bin/bash
#
# $1 is the calling fax machine's station ID
# $2 is filename
mutt -n -f /dev/null -F ~/.muttrc -a $2 -s "Fax from $1" user@domain.
com < /dev/null
```

Be sure to replace `user@domain.com` with a valid e-mail address. Lastly, create the file `.muttrc` in the home directory and add these lines:

```
set from = 'sender@domain'
set realname = 'Organization or business name'
set folder = /dev/null
```

Received faxes will now be sent to the specified user with the calling fax machine's station ID.

 Many scripting languages like Perl, Python, and Ruby have libraries that allow you to send e-mails. Feel free to try replacing `emailfax.sh` with your own e-mail sender script.

See also

> ▸ Refer to the *Sending faxes* recipe in this chapter

Basic text-to-speech with mod_flite

Sometimes you need a fast, simple, and free text-to-speech implementation for some quick testing. In FreeSWITCH you can use `mod_flite` for simple TTS testing. While it is not suitable for professional, production environments, it meets the criteria of being quick, easy, and free.

Getting ready

Other than a phone and a text editor there is not much you need. Keep in mind that on Windows the `mod_flite` module is pre-built but it is not automatically loaded. On Linux/Unix systems you will need to perform a few steps listed below.

How to do it...

If you are in Windows then skip to step 3. If you have Linux/Unix then follow these steps to enable `mod_flite`:

1. Open `modules.conf` in the FreeSWITCH source and uncomment the line with `#asr_tts/mod_flite` by removing the # at the beginning of the line.

2. Save and exit. Run the `install` command:

   make mod_flite-install

3. If you wish to have `mod_flite` load by default when FreeSWITCH starts then open `conf/autoload_configs/modules.conf.xml` and uncomment this line:

```
<!-- <load module="mod_flite"/> -->
```

4. Save and exit. At `fs_cli`, issue the command `load mod_flite`.

At this point `mod_flite` is now active and ready to be used. Now let's add a simple diaplan extension that will let us test it:

1. Open `conf/dialplan/default/01_Custom.xml` and add this extension:

```
<extension name="mod_flite example">
  <condition field="destination_number" expression="^(5008)">
    <action application="answer"/>
    <action application="sleep" data="500"/>
    <action application="speak"
        data="flite|kal|Hello world. This is a FreeSWITCH test."/>
  </condition>
</extension>
```

2. Save the file and exit. Issue the `reloadxml` command from `fs_cli` or press *F6*.

You are now ready to test. Simply dial *5008* and listen to the voice.

How it works...

FreeSWITCH has a `speak` dialplan application that is used to access any installed TTS engine. It accepts pipe-delimited arguments. Note the line we used in the dialplan:

```
<action application="speak"
        data="flite|kal|Hello world. This is a FreeSWITCH test."/>
```

The first argument is the name of the TTS engine. The second argument is the name of the voice for the TTS engine. The last argument is the actual text to be spoken. The `sleep` app is optional, however, in many cases it is necessary to pause momentarily after answering a call to allow the media streams to be established.

 Don't confuse the dialplan `speak` application (TTS) with the `say` application! The `say` application is convenient for saying things like dates, times, numbers, currency, etc. using the pre-recorded sound prompts.

Flite comes with four voices that you can try out: `awb`, `kal`, `rms`, and `slt`.

See also

▶ Refer to the *Advanced text-to-speech with mod_tts_commandline* recipe in this chapter

Advanced text-to-speech with mod_tts_commandline

The **Text-to-speech (TTS)** applications vary in their quality, complexity, and price. One thing most high-end TTS engines have in common, though, is a command line interface for generating audio from text. FreeSWITCH's mod_tts_commandline module is designed to take advantage of this. While it is completely possible to create a separate module for each engine—and indeed this is the case for mod_flite—it is convenient to utilize a more generic interface that is somewhat agnostic to the exact TTS engine being used.

In this recipe we will install mod_tts_commandline and then download a free TTS engine that has a command line interface to use with it. We will also show command line examples of using some commercial TTS engines.

Getting ready

This recipe has a few prerequisites. The most important one is to get a copy of the freeswitch-contrib git repository. The "contrib repo" as community members call it, contains a number of items freely given back to the FreeSWITCH community as a whole. One of these will assist us with installing the Pico TTS engine that is a part of the Android project. The basic command to clone the git repo is:

```
git clone git://git.freeswitch.org/freeswitch-contrib.git
```

The subdirectory created will simply be referred to as freeswitch-contrib.

 Git is a popular revision control system used by many projects, including the Linux kernel. If you are unfamiliar with it we suggest you visit this wiki page to get started: http://wiki.freeswitch.org/wiki/Git_Tips.

How to do it...

If you are in Windows then skip to step 3. If you have Linux/Unix then follow these steps to enable mod_tts_commandline:

1. Open modules.conf in the FreeSWITCH source and uncomment the line with #asr_tts/mod_tts_commandline by removing the # at the beginning of the line.

2. Save and exit. Run the `install` command:

```
make mod_tts_commandline-install
```

3. If you wish to have `mod_tts_commandline` load by default when FreeSWITCH starts then open `conf/autoload_configs/modules.conf.xml` and uncomment this line:

```
<!-- <load module="mod_tts_commandline"/> -->
```

4. Save the file and close. Open `conf/autoload_configs/tts_commandline.xml` and locate the line beginning with `<param name="command"`.... Change the line to this:

```
<param name="command" value="pico2wave -w ${file} ${text} "/>
```

5. (For Windows use `pico2wave.exe` instead of `pico2wave`).

6. Save the file and exit.

At this point `mod_tts_commandline` is now compiled and is almost ready for use. Next let's build the pico TTS engine. Linux/Unix users follow these steps:

1. Change directory to `freeswitch-contrib/grmt/svox pico/svox/pico` (note the space between "svox" and "pico")

2. Execute these shell commands:

```
sh ./autogen.sh
./configure
make && make install
```

Windows users will need to locate the appropriate solution file in `freeswitch-contrib\grmt\mod_tts_commandline` for Windows:

- `mod_tts_commandline.2008.vcproj` – Visual Studio 2008
- `mod_tts_commandline.2010.vcxproj` – Visual Studio 2010

Open the appropriate solution file and then rebuild.

You will now have the `pico2wave` (or `pico2wave.exe` in Windows) command-line utility.

Now let's add a simple diaplan extension that will let us use `tts_commandline` and `pico`:

1. Open `conf/dialplan/default/01_Custom.xml` and add this extension:

    ```
    <extension name="mod_tts_commandline example">
      <condition field="destination_number" expression="^(5010)">
        <action application="answer"/>
        <action application="sleep" data="500"/>
        <action application="speak" data="tts_commandline|pico|Hello
        world. This is a FreeSWITCH test."/>
      </condition>
    </extension>
    ```

2. Save the file and exit. Issue the `reloadxml` command from `fs_cli` or press *F6*.

3. At `fs_cli`, issue the command `load mod_tts_commandline`.

You are now ready to test. Simply dial *5010* and listen to the voice.

How it works...

There are several elements that interact to make this work. We first built `mod_tts_commandline` (just like we would in any other FreeSWITCH module) and then configured it to use `pico2wave` or `pico2wave.exe`. Next, we installed the `pico2wave` command line utility. Lastly we created a simple dialplan to call the speak application and read our text.

There's more...

The really interesting part of `mod_tts_commandline` occurs in the configuration file. The command parameter tells `mod_tts_commandline` what to execute when the `speak` application is called. Read on for some tricks that you can do with `tts_commandline.conf.xml`.

Modifying the audio stream

It is possible to use an intermediate program, such as **Sound eXchange (SoX)**, to modify the audio that is output from `pico2wave`. An example of this is to resample the audio. By default, `pico2wave` generates mono 16 kHz wave files. If the audio you hear from `mod_tts_commandline` sounds too fast or too slow then try resampling with SoX. Open `conf/autoload_configs/tts_commandline.conf.xml` and modify the `command` parameter. For Linux/Unix use this entry:

```
<param name="command" value="pico2wave -w /tmp/$$.wav ${text} && sox /
tmp/$$.wav -r ${rate} ${file} && rm /tmp/$$.wav"/>
```

For Windows use this entry:

```
<param name="command" value="pico2wave.exe -w c:\\tmp\\$$.wav ${text}
&& sox.exe C:\\tmp\\$$.wav -r ${rate} ${file} && del c:\\tmp\\$$.
wav"/>
```

(Be sure that `C:\tmp` exists, or use an appropriate folder on your Windows system.)

You will need to issue `reloadxml` or press *F6* at `fs_cli` as well `reload mod_tts_commandline` for the changes to take effect.

> SoX can perform an amazing array of effects on an audio stream.
> Learn more at `http://sox.sourceforge.net/`.

Other TTS engines

The FreeSWITCH community has tested `mod_tts_commandline` with a number of commercial TTS engines, mostly under Linux environments. If you have one of the following TTS engines then use one of the command parameter entries listed below. In some cases you will need to tweak your command line parameters. A simple way to test is to manually run your command and generate a wave file on disk, such as `/tmp/test.wav`. Then use a simple dialplan to playback the file:

```
<condition field="destination_number" expression="^(5010)">
  <action application="answer"/>
  <action application="sleep" data="500"/>
  <action application="playback" data="/tmp/test.wav"/>
</condition>
```

This is much easier than making repeated changes to `tts_commandline.conf.xml` and reloading `mod_tts_commandline`. Once you have perfected your command line syntax then update the configuration file and test.

Configuration file examples

The configuration file examples are as follows:

- **Festival**: It is the same engine used in `mod_flite`:

  ```
  <param name="command" value="echo ${text} | text2wave -f ${rate} >
  ${file}"/>
  ```

- **Cepstral**:

  ```
  <param name="command" value="swift -n ${voice} ${text} -o
  ${file}"/>
  ```

- **Loquendo**:

  ```
  <param name="command" value="echo ${text} | TTSFileGenerator
  -v${voice} -o${file}"/>
  ```

See also

- Refer to the *Basic text-to-speech with mod_flite* earlier in this chapter

Listening to live calls with telecast

Sometimes you will wish to listen to calls in progress. It is not always easy to "catch" a specific call. FreeSWITCH includes a simple interface that let's you listen in on a call with only a browser and an MP3 player such as iTunes. This feature is called **telecast**.

Getting ready

Be sure to complete the steps in the *Using the built-in web interface* recipe in this chapter before attempting to use the telecast feature. You will also need a browser and speakers or headphones in order to listen in during a phone call.

How to do it...

Start by enabling mod_shout, which is what handles the audio stream. Windows users skip to step 3. Linux/Unix users start with these steps:

1. Open modules.conf in the FreeSWITCH source and uncomment the line with #formats/mod_shout by removing the # at the beginning of the line.

2. Save and exit. Build the module with this command:

   make mod_shout-install

3. Set mod_shout to load by default when FreeSWITCH starts. Open conf/autoload_configs/modules.conf.xml and uncomment this line

   ```
   <!-- <load module="mod_shout"/> -->
   ```

4. Save the file and exit.

5. At the fs_cli issue the command load mod_shout.

At this point the telecast API is loaded. Browse to `http://<ip_addr>:8080/webabi/telecast/index` to pull up the list of active calls. The default username is "freeswitch" and the default password is "works". Here is an example of a call in progress.Refer the following screenshot:

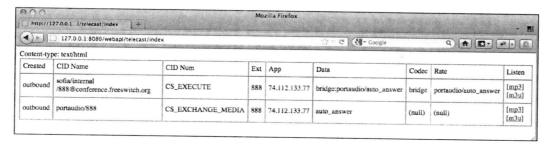

Click one of the links in the **Listen** column, where **mp3** will open your computer's default MP3 player and **m3u** will open iTunes if it is installed on your system. The audio of the call will stream as long as the call is in progress.

How it works...

While `mod_xml_rpc` provides the Web interface, it is `mod_shout` that provides the ability to stream audio. In fact, the actual HTML code of this telecast interface resides in `mod_shout.c`, however it still requires the web server functionality provided by `mod_xml_rpc` in order to work.

This simple interface is just an example of what is possible with the `telecast` interface. It is not dynamic nor is it AJAX-enabled. You will have to refresh the browser to see an updated call list. The `telecast` interface can be interfaced with a more traditional web server (Apache, nginx, Lighttpd) to create a more sophisticated on-line application.

See also

▸ Refer to the *Using the built-in web interface* recipe earlier in this chapter

Recording calls

Many enterprises need to record calls for quality control purposes. This recipe describes how you can record inbound and outbound calls on your FreeSWITCH server. If you need assistance in getting calls into and out of your FreeSWITCH system, refer to *Inbound DID calls* and *Outgoing calls* both in *Chapter 1*.

Most countries and localities have laws relating to the recording of phone calls. Always consult a licensed legal professional in your jurisdiction before you start recording phone calls.

Getting ready

Recording calls is actually very simple. All you need is a text editor so that you can add a few lines to your dialplan.

How to do it...

The FreeSWITCH dialplan application `record_session` is used for recording calls, whether they are inbound or outbound. (Call direction does not affect the `record_session` application.)

For inbound calls it is easiest to enable recording right on the `Local_Extension`. Follow the steps:

1. Open `conf/dialplan/default.xml` and locate the `Local_Extension` dialplan entry. Add these lines right after the line with the `answer` application:

```
<action application="set" data="record_file_name={recordings_
dir}/${strftime(%Y-%m-%d-%H-%M-%S)}_${uuid}.wav" inline="true"/>
<action application="record_session" data="{record_file_name}"/>
```

2. Save the file, then run `fs_cli` and press *F6* or issue the `reloadxml` command.

Now any call made to a local extension will be recorded. (This includes internal calls from one phone extension to another.)

For outbound calls we need to do something a bit different because we don't necessarily know that the call will actually be answered.

1. Open the dialplan file that contains your outbound route. Add these lines right before your `bridge` application:

```
<action application="set" data="record_file_name={recordings_
dir}/${strftime(%Y-%m-%d-%H-%M-%S)}_${uuid}.wav" inline="true"/>
<action application="export" data="execute_on_answer=record_
session {record_file_name}"/>
```

2. Save the file, then run `fs_cli` and press *F6* or issue the `reloadxml` command.

Now any answered call made through this gateway will be recorded.

How it works...

The `record_session` application will record the audio on the channel. Technically, the `record_session` application is only running on one leg of the call. In the inbound example, it is running on the called leg (B leg). In the outbound example it is running on the calling leg (A leg). The `record_session` application records audio in both directions and therefore the entire call is recorded.

The filename is stored in the channel variable `record_file_name`. We piece together several bits of information to create the full path:

- ► `${recordings_dir}`: By default this gets set to `${base_dir}/recordings/`
- ► `strftime(%Y-%m-%d-%H-%M-%S)`: This produces a timestamp in the format of YYYY-MM-DD-hh-mm-ss
- ► `${uuid}.wav`: This adds the calls' unique ID to the filename

The net result is that our file has a complete and unique path and file name. For example:

```
/usr/local/freeswitch/recordings/2012-02-21-13-34-18_ca806474-1c30-
4052-b366-17f2e9287cb2.wav
```

> The `strftime` API is very handy for getting the current date and time in various formats. It uses the format strings found in the standard Unix `strftime` command. You can experiment with it at `fs_cli`. Try issuing different commands like `strftime` and `strftime %Y-%m-%d-%H-%M-%S` to see what you get.

There's more...

You may have noticed that the `Local_Extension` has a curious entry:

```
<action application="bind_meta_app" data="2 b s record_
session::$${recordings_dir}/${caller_id_number}.${strftime(%Y-%m-%d-
%H-%M-%S)}.wav"/>
```

By default, a user who receives a call can manually enable call recording by pressing *2. By itself this a handy feature, however in the case where we automatically record all calls this feature is irrelevant. A much more useful feature would be the ability to turn off the call recording. This can easily be done by adding a few more lines to our dialplan. Note that we only want our telephone user (what we usually call an "agent") to be able to control the call recording, which means we need to enable a key combination only on the agent's leg of the call. The agent is the A leg on an outbound call and is the B leg on the inbound call. Fortunately, we already have separate dialplan entries for each call type. We simply need to add the appropriate `bind_meta_app` in each case.

For inbound calls we just need to replace the `bind_meta_app` entry mentioned above. Open `conf/dialplan/default.xml` and replace the "curious entry" with this line:

```
<action application="bind_meta_app" data="2 b s execute_
extension::stop_record_${dialed_extension}"/>
```

Save the file and exit. For outbound calls, open the dialplan file to which you added the `record_session` application. Right before the bridge application add this line:

```
<action application="bind_meta_app" data="2 a s execute_
extension::stop_record_${caller_id_number}"/>
```

Save the file and exit. The last step is to create a new dialplan file that will handle the "stop recording" action that we have implemented. Create a new file in `conf/dialplan/` called `recording.xml` and add these lines:

```
<include>
  <context="recordings">
    <extension name="Stop Recording"/>
      <condition field="destination_number"
      expression="^stop_recording_(.*)">
        <action application="log" data="WARNING Agent $1 has stopped
        a recording"/>
        <action application="stop_record_session"
        data="${record_filename}"/>
        <action application="set" data="res=${uuid_broadcast ${uuid}
        ivr/ivr-recording_stopped.wav both}"/>
      </condition>
    </extension>
  </context>
</include>
```

Save the file and exit. Open `fs_cli` and press *F6* or issue the `reloadxml` command. Now test the feature. Have an agent press **2* on an active call. The agent and caller/callee should hear, "recording stopped." The console will show the `stop_record_session` application being executed. The call recording will now be stopped.

See also

▸ Refer to the *Incoming DID calls* and the *Outgoing calls* recipes in *Chapter 1*

Index

Thank you for buying
FreeSWITCH Cookbook

About Packt Publishing

Packt, pronounced 'packed', published its first book "*Mastering phpMyAdmin for Effective MySQL Management*" in April 2004 and subsequently continued to specialize in publishing highly focused books on specific technologies and solutions.

Our books and publications share the experiences of your fellow IT professionals in adapting and customizing today's systems, applications, and frameworks. Our solution based books give you the knowledge and power to customize the software and technologies you're using to get the job done. Packt books are more specific and less general than the IT books you have seen in the past. Our unique business model allows us to bring you more focused information, giving you more of what you need to know, and less of what you don't.

Packt is a modern, yet unique publishing company, which focuses on producing quality, cutting-edge books for communities of developers, administrators, and newbies alike. For more information, please visit our website: www.packtpub.com.

About Packt Open Source

In 2010, Packt launched two new brands, Packt Open Source and Packt Enterprise, in order to continue its focus on specialization. This book is part of the Packt Open Source brand, home to books published on software built around Open Source licences, and offering information to anybody from advanced developers to budding web designers. The Open Source brand also runs Packt's Open Source Royalty Scheme, by which Packt gives a royalty to each Open Source project about whose software a book is sold.

Writing for Packt

We welcome all inquiries from people who are interested in authoring. Book proposals should be sent to author@packtpub.com. If your book idea is still at an early stage and you would like to discuss it first before writing a formal book proposal, contact us; one of our commissioning editors will get in touch with you.

We're not just looking for published authors; if you have strong technical skills but no writing experience, our experienced editors can help you develop a writing career, or simply get some additional reward for your expertise.

open source
community experience distilled

FreeSWITCH 1.0.6

ISBN: 978-1-847199-96-6   Paperback: 320 pages

Build robust high performance telephony systems using FreeSWITCH

1. Install and configure a complete telephony system of your own even if you are using FreeSWITCH for the first time

2. In-depth discussions of important concepts like the dialplan, user directory, and the powerful FreeSWITCH Event Socket

3. The first ever book on FreeSWITCH, packed with real-world examples for Linux/Unix systems, Mac OSX, and Windows, along with useful screenshots and diagrams

Building Telephony Systems with OpenSIPS 1.6

ISBN: 978-1-849510-74-5   Paperback: 284 pages

Build scalable and robust telephony systems using SIP

1. Build a VoIP Provider based on the SIP Protocol

2. Cater to scores of subscribers efficiently with a robust telephony system based in pure SIP

3. Gain a competitive edge using the most scalable VoIP technology

4. Learn how to avoid pitfalls using precise billing

5. Packed with rich practical examples and case studies on the latest OpenSIPS version 1.6

Please check **www.PacktPub.com** for information on our titles